PLACE-NAME DETECTIVE
Bedwyr Lewis Jones

PLACE-NAME
DETECTIVE

Bedwyr Lewis Jones

translated by
Anthony Lias

© Text: Eleri Wyn Jones
First published in Welsh: *Enwau* (1991), *Yn ei Elfen* (1992)
© English translation: Anthony Lias

ISBN: 978-1-84527-145-9

Cover design/Cartoons: Alan Jôs

Published with the financial support
of the Welsh Books Council.

Published by
Gwasg Carreg Gwalch, 12 Iard yr Orsaf, Llanrwst,
Wales LL26 0EH.
Tel: 01492 642031   Fax: 01492 641502
E-mail: books@carreg-gwalch.com
Website: www.carreg-gwalch.com

CONTENTS

BEDWYR LEWIS JONES
An introduction by Gwyn Thomas

The sudden death of Professor Bedwyr Lewis Jones at the end of the summer of 1992 shocked the Welsh nation. In a moving elegy to him, one that is full of resonances from the long tradition of poetic lament in Welsh, Gerallt Lloyd Owen said that he was known to everyone by his first name:

a Bedwyr gan bawb ydoedd.

This academic was well-known, and not a name that had to be disinterred from the pages of books and journals known only to fellow academics. There is a tradition in Wales for Welsh academics to take an active part in the cultural, communal, and political life of their country. The first professor of Welsh at the Univeristy College in Bangor, Sir John Morris-Jones, was the first eminent scholar whose name was familiar to a great number of people in Wales. He was much respected, but was also enthusiastically criticized by some of the more ardent adherents to a false tradition in eisteddfodic circles. His successors in the chair carried on the tradition of being active in the public life of Wales. John Morris-Jones' immediate successor, Sir Ifor Williams, whose pioneering scholarship in the earliest and then largely unilluminated period of Welsh literature, is still one of the great feats of Celtic studies, began to take an interest in Welsh place-names. When John Morris-Jones heard of this he is said to have told him, 'Only a fool dabbles in place-names'. At the time there was some justification for saying this, because a large part of the commentaries on Welsh place-names were, more often than not, guesswork. Ifor Williams and others began to establish a dependable method of dealing with such names.

This involved a great deal of research into records that noted the earlier forms of places. Such research revealed that many names had been corrupted in common speech so that the true explanations of their meanings were very different from what seemed to be apparent to interested, but untrained, elucidators.

In addition to this research one needed to be a philologist, as the term was; one who could work out the meanings of, in this case, Welsh words by noting their contexts over the centuries, and by comparing them with words in related Celtic languages, such as the sister-languages of Welsh, namely Cornish and Breton, or cousin-languages, namely Irish, Gaelic and Manx, whenever this was possible. In the case of Welsh, too, one had to consider borrowings from other languages, especially from Latin and English. For example, the explanation for the mountain peak called `Cnicht', in north Wales, is based on an old English pronunciation of the word `knight'. The man who explained the meaning of this peak was Professor Melville Richards, who was professor of Welsh at Bangor from 1965 to 1973.

Of all Welsh academics who have dealt with place-names, Melville Richards is by far the most eminent. He gathered examples of place-names from written records for many years and his immense collection of data is now deposited at the library of the University at Bangor. All serious students of Welsh place-names in the period since his death are indebted to this invaluable collection, which is now available as computer data. Bedwyr was the first to acknowledge his debt to this collection, but he went on to do his own extensive researches in his own way, drawing on his own great store of knowledge and training in the study of Welsh and linguistics, and of literature and, on occasion, his explanations would differ from those offered by Professor Richards.

Professor Richards was himself an academic who took part in a popular and original television series (`Lloffa' - `*gleaning*') that sought to explain matters relating to Welsh culture, in a general sense, to ordinary viewers, but it was Bedwyr who went on to become the elucidator par excellence of a vast variety of topics such as place-names, words, sayings, and literature. He was the ideal person for the work because he was a precise and painstaking academic, and also a natural, as well as a trained, educator. He took delight in explaining often very intricate matters lucidly and interestingly; in this respect he was a worthy student and follower of his own professor, Thomas Parry. In fact, his lectures on Welsh language, literature and culture were both appealing and entertaining, a fact that accounts for his popularity as a teacher within and outside the walls of his college, and as an eminently successful broadcaster and television presenter.

But there was another reason for his success as an educator; he was by nature a man of the people, and one who had been graced with a substantial dose of common sense, that indefinable but very real commodity. He knew what would make the complex clear and comprehensible to ordinary people – as well as to bright students. He was always receptive to the wisdom and richness of the talk of civilized (not necessarily learned) people from all walks of life and he was a great scribbler of unusual words and expressions that he heard from time to time. He set these things down in his small, neat hand in a series of notebooks. Here is an example of his coming across an unusual use of a word: he was lecturing on place-names in a class in Llangefni, Anglesey, and dealing with the name `Bangor'. He explained that `bangor' originally meant a stout rod in a wattle hedge or fence used to strengthen the structure, and that the meaning extended from this to the structure itself, and that it came to be used for a monastic cell. The Bangor in north Wales takes its name from such a monastic cell. Someone asked a question, and then another member of the class said to that person (in Welsh, of course), "But you use one of these every day, your stick for driving cattle - `bangor'!". Bedwyr was delighted with this discovery and, as always, shared his delight with his friends.

I remember well his delight in discovering fragments of real antiquity in the everyday language of people. Such discoveries depended, to a large degree, on his own knowledge of the past, a knowledge which provided him with a context that those using old expressions or words did not know. He was very excited – and excitement about discoveries and new insights were of the essence of his learning and knowledge – when he heard someone in Powys refer to the sharp east wind there as `wind from the old Pengwern'. He immediately recognized `Pengwern' as the old Welsh name for the region around modern Shrewsbury, and the name for an ancient Welsh court in that area. The memory of the old Pengwern had survived in Powys, in the speech of some of its people, for centuries. He was equally excited when he heard someone in his native Anglesey refer to the social services department in the county in this way, `Caiff Berffro dalu' (`Berffro can pay'). He realized that deep in the consciousness or, may be, in the subconscious of this speaker was the feeling that the centre of some kind of government in Anglesey was not Llangefni, but Aberffraw, the seat of the ancient Welsh princes. The memory of the medieval Welsh court had lodged itself in the speech of some of the people of Anglesey until the twentieth century. Such debris retained in the living language, spoken by people in their patch for hundreds of years, fascinated him. We are now at a stage when this kind of richness retained in the continuity of a language is coming to an end – in English and Welsh. The ease of movement of people from one place to another, and the overwhelming influence of the media erases such riches from our speech. Bedwyr would have been delighted with the excavation of an old Welsh court just outside Niwbwrch in a field which had always been known to the locals as – `Cae Llys' (*'court field'*)!

It is important that Bedwyr's study of place-names is now translated into English, because such a study requires the attention of an expert, and the study of place-names seems to draw to it the consideration of many persons who are anything but experts. This is an authoritative as well as a most entertaining study, and one that will reveal to the reader Bedwyr's unique and warm personality.

Gwyn Thomas

11

PREFACE

It seems likely that everyone who read the place-name articles of the late Professor Bedwyr Lewis Jones in the *Western Mail*, or listened to his radio broadcasts, will have had his or her particular favourites. To some extent this is certainly true in the case of the present translator, who was first captivated by the professor's writings as presented in the compilation *Enwau* ('Names') by Carreg Gwalch in 1991. But it's equally true to say that favouritism has played little or no part in the selection offered here. Since it is intended mainly – though not exclusively – for non-Welsh speakers, common sense dictated that sufficient space should be given to those place-names probably best known to them: Cardiff, Carmarthen, Prestatyn etc. That said, however, it would have been wrong to exclude more 'out of the way' names such as Esgobaeth Brân, Gabalfa and others like them. The professor's searching gaze fell on these, too, and his explanations display all the shrewdness, charm and humour that were his unique trademark. He knew that *all* place-names have much to tell us, whatever their outward 'status'. I can only hope that the present selection does adequate justice to a learned scholar who was also a naturally gifted communicator.

It only remains to be noted that the use of 'we', 'our', 'us' etc. in the book refers to the Welsh people, for whom the pieces were originally intended. But I also wish to thank Myrddin ap Dafydd for his kindness in accepting my proposal to undertake the translations, and for his patience and encouragement over many months.

Anthony Lias

WHY WALES? WHY CYMRU?

Cymru is the name of our country in Welsh, but *Wales* in English. Both names have an interesting history.

Wales, to begin with. That goes back ultimately to a word *walh* or *wealh* meaning 'foreign, foreigner' in Germanic, the early language from which sprang English and German. *Walh* was the word used by Germanic speakers on the continent around 2000 years ago for a person whose language they didn't understand.

Thus *walh* was used of anyone speaking Latin. That is why *Walloon* is the present-day name for those people in Belgium who speak French, which is a late form of Latin. The meaning of *wall* at the beginning of the name is 'foreign', since in the eyes of the early Germanic people the Latin of the *Belgae* was a foreign language.

Britain was full of people speaking in foreign tongues – some in Latin and a great many more in Brythonic, a Celtic tongue. The whole lot were *walh*, 'foreign', or – in the plural – *wealas*, 'foreigners'. 'Welsh' and 'Wales' are much later forms of *wealas*. In the eyes of the early English, we – the Welsh – were foreigners, even in our own country!

The same thing was true as regards the people of Cornwall. *Cornwealas* was the English name for them – i.e. the *wealas* or foreigners who lived in the 'Horn of land' or peninsula. Later on *Cornwealas* changed to Cornwall.

The *wall* at the end of *Cornwall* is the same word at root as the *wal* at the beginning of *Wales* and the *wall* at the beginning of *Walloon*. It is also identical with the *wal* in *walnut* – a nut that was *foreign* to Britain.

The source of *Cymry*, our own name for ourselves, is completely different. *Cymry* is the plural of *Cymro*; and *Cymro* goes back to a word in very early Welsh – and before that in Brythonic – which was a combination of *com* and *bro*, the latter word meaning 'region, territory within a boundary'. The original meaning of the name *Cymro* was 'a man from the same region, a man from a country or district within a boundary'. So the meaning of *Cymry* is 'people from the same country, compatriots'.

At one time a *b* came after the *m* in the name, but *mb* changed to *m* by around the year 600. The *mb* has remained in the Latin form *Cambria*, and from the Latin *Cambria* comes *Cambrian* in English – a term which is used, for example, to denote very ancient rocks.

The *mb* also survives in the names *Cumbria* and *Cumberland* in the north of England. These names are

14

forms of *Cymry*. Long ago Cumberland was a land of the Cymry, before the Cymry there were conquered by the English. At that time the people of Cumbria and those of our own Wales saw themselves as compatriots. We too continue to call the north of England and the south of Scotland 'the Old North' – *our* Old North.

ABERAFAN
(Aberavon)

Aber is the Welsh word for a place where a river flows into the sea, or where a smaller river joins a larger one. It is a very common element at the beginning of place-names in Wales. It's also found in parts of Scotland – for example, in *Aberdeen* at the mouth of the river Don, and in Arbroath. *Aberbrothog* was the old form of the latter – namely the place where Bannock Burn flows into the sea.

Aberafan is the place where the river Afan has its outlet to the sea. The forms *Afan* and *Afen* occur early on for the river-name, but no one rightly knows how to explain them.

Some have supposed that *Afan* was a form of the word *afon*, 'river'. The naming *Ecclesia Abbona*, i.e. 'Church on the river', occurs as early as 1348, and the English antiquary John Leland mentions *Aber-Avon* in 1536-1539. But although the form *Aberavon* is very old, it's a false form. The correct name is *Aberafan*.

Port Talbot (i.e. the docks at Aberafan Harbour) is a late name. It was coined around 1836, when the docks were newly built to export coal and iron from the estuary of the river Afan. The docks took their name from the Talbots, an English family who had inherited the old estates of Margam and Pen-rhys through marriage. *Port Talbot* was just one of the English names containing *Port-* which were coined during the nineteenth century, when new ports were being built along the coasts of Wales.

Others include *Port Penrhyn* in Bangor, the harbour

which was constructed for the export of slate from Penrhyn Quarry. Then there is *Port Dinorwig* in Y Felinheli* (export of slate from Dinorwig Quarry). And there's also *Porthmadog* (Portmadoc), which was named after the local tradition of Ynys Madog – an island from where the twelfth century adventurer Madog ab Owain Gwynedd sailed to discover America – and which is also connected to William Alexander Maddocks, the man who caused an embankment or cob to be raised across Traeth Mawr ('great strand') and then later built a harbour there.

Another foreign name of the same type is *Portmeirion*, the name of the pseudo-Italian village which Clough Williams-Ellis created in the vicinity of Traeth Bach ('little strand') near *Penrhyndeudraeth*, the peninsula between Traeth Bach and Traeth Mawr – i.e. 'peninsula of the two (*dau*) strands'.

* Literally 'salt-water mill' or 'tidal mill' – translator's note

ABERHONDDU
(Brecon)

We have seen that *aber* is the word for the place where a river flows into the sea or where a smaller river joins a larger one. It's the second meaning that applies in *Aberhonddu*. The name designates the place where the river Honddu joins the Usk.

But what about the river-name itself? It's *Honddu* today – and in fact has been for 200 years and more. But go further back than this and you see that the old form was *Hoddni* – *Hodd* representing the word *hawdd* at the beginning, the same word that means 'pleasant', 'pleasing' (and which appears in *hawddfyd*, 'ease'). *Hoddni* describes a fine or pleasant river.

In spoken Welsh it was possible for *ddn* in the middle of a word to change into *ndd* – a change which is called transposition, or 'metathesis'. There's the name *Rhoddni*, which in the course of time changed into *Rhondda*; in the same way *Hoddni* changed into *Honddi*, and subsequently the final *i* became *u* – probably because someone thought that *du* ('black') was the last element.

In English the name is *Brecon*. A man called Brychan was king of this area in the fifth century, a man of Irish stock. In the early period of Welsh, the ending *-iog* could be added to a name of a person so as to create a name for the land belonging to that person. The adding of *-iog* to *Brychan* gave *Brycheiniog*, meaning 'land of Brychan'.

But what about the form *Brecon*? That is the English

Brecon castle

form of *Brychan* – and the English form of *Brycheiniog* is
Brecknock*.

* Brecknock*shire*, or Brecon*shire*, denotes the county
– translator's note

ABERTAWE
(Swansea)

Abertawe is the place where the river Tawe flows into the sea. *Abertawy* was the old form, because *Tawy* – with -*y* at the end – was the old name of the river.

What about *Swansea*, the English name for Abertawe? The simple fact is that this name is not English at all in origin but Scandinavian, being a combination of the Scandinavian personal name *Sveinn* and the element *ey* meaning 'island'.

Swansea's indoor market – famous for its local produce

A thousand years ago the people living along the coast of Wales were well aware of the men of Scandinavia – the Vikings. They were a plague to coastal folk, sailing in their sharp-prowed ships from their kingdoms around Dublin and in the northern isles of Scotland, making attacks on inhabited centres, plundering monasteries and churches, and snatching locals to sell them as slaves.

It was some of these Vikings who named the mouth of the river Tawe 'Sveinn's island' after one of their leaders. At that time the course of the river near its mouth was very different from what it is today. Some sort of island existed there, and the river forked around it.

When the Normans came to the area sometime towards 1100 or soon afterwards and built a town and a castle, they could have adopted the – geographical – Welsh name *Abertawe* ('mouth of the Tawe'). But they didn't do so. Instead they accepted the Scandinavian name and, in the course of time, that turned into *Swansea*.

ADSOFL-WEN

This is the name of a farm in the vicinity of Mynachlog-ddu, Pembrokeshire. There is also an *Adsol-wen* in the vicinity of Nebo, a village in Ceredigion. So what about the name itself?

In the month of June, farmers mow the grass for hay – and note that the Welsh word *lladd*, not *torri* here, is used for 'mow'. Subsequently the grass for hay grows again, leading to the *adladd* or *adlodd*, 'second mowing'. Later in the summer comes the corn-harvest. Then the corn is cut (*torri*) leaving stumps of straw. The word for these stumps is *sofl* – 'stubble' in English. If the stubble-land is left for the remainder of the year without being ploughed, that's the *atsofl* or *adsofl* – harvested cornland subsequently left untouched.

In the spoken tongue there is a tendency for the *f* before the *l* to disappear: for *adsofl* to give the form *adsol*. And so we have the *Adsofl-wen* near Mynachlog-ddu, and the *Adsol-wen* near Nebo in Ceredigion. Stubble land, white – *(g)wen* – in appearance, gave both places their names.

It's also possible for the *d* in *Adsol* to be lost. *Asol* occurs as a form for *Adsol* in parts of south-western Wales; and it's often found in field names – sometimes in the form *Rasol*, i.e. *Yr Asol*. I have also seen *Yr Asol-wen* and *Rasol-wen* as versions of the name *Adsol-wen* in Ceredigion.

Since I'm talking about the word *sofl*, 'stubble', it's as well to add that this, probably, is what occurs in the name

Resolfen in Glamorgan. *Rhos* is the first part of this name in old documents – *Rhos-solfen*, i.e. moorland that was once stubble-land. In speech, *f* and *l* in (an original) *Rhosoflen* have been transposed to give *Rhosolfen*, and this becomes *Rosolfen* and *Resolfen*.

An old picture postcard of Colwyn Bay pier

BAE COLWYN
(Colwyn Bay)

Bae Colwyn is the second-largest town in northern Wales, after Wrecsam (Wrexham).

It's not hard to explain the *Bae* part of the name. The Welsh version of the English *bay*, it was tacked on to *Colwyn* in order to tell visitors from England that the place boasted a fine beach. The addition dates from the Sixties and Seventies of the nineteenth century, when our northern coastline was beginning to sprout holiday centres.

What about *Colwyn* itself? There was a word *colwyn* in Welsh whose original meaning was 'young animal'. It was used of a young dog – and especially of a male one. 'Pretty little doggies to amuse the women,' was the pleasing definition of *Colwyn* by Thomas Wiliems of Trefriw (1545/6 – 1622) in his dictionary. The word also appears in an old saying, 'Happy is the little dog on his master's knee.' But what has all this to do with the name of a town in the north?

Well, in Welsh you often find rivers named after animals. There's a river Twrch ('boar'), for example, in both Ystalyfera and Llanuwchllyn; a river Hwch ('sow') near Llanberis; while *banw*, a word for a young pig, lies behind the names of the river *Banw* (in Montgomeryshire), and – ultimately – of the *Aman* (Carmarthenshire) and the *Ogwen* (Bethesda, Arfon).

Colwyn also came to denote streams or rivulets. There are several of them – one rising on the slopes of Yr Wyddfa (Snowdon) and flowing down to Beddgelert, one flowing into the river Cerist near Caersws, and another into the river Efyrnwy in Dyffryn Meifod.

There is also a river Colwyn in the district of Llanelian-yn-Rhos (another name for it being the river Penmaen). This river name became that of a township and then, in due course, that of the towns, Old Colwyn and Bae Colwyn.

Y BARRI
(Barry)

The name of the town *Barri* in Glamorgan is a difficult one to explain. The reason is that there are variations in the earliest forms available to us in old documents – forms dating back to around 1200. Sometimes you get *Barri*, with an *-i* sound at the end; but sometimes you get *Barren*.

Suppose for the moment that Barren was the original name. The final *n* could be lost. That happened in the name Rhos Sulien in Gower, the *n* dropping off to give us *Rhosili*. If the *n* in Barren was lost, *Barre* could easily change to *Barri* – and the change is a possible one.

But what would be the meaning of *Barri*? There was an old Welsh word *bar*, with a short *a*, meaning 'top', 'point', 'summit'. This is what appears in the village name *Crug-y-bar* in Carmarthenshire and in the *Berwyn* mountain names. With *-en* on the end, *barren* would give a word for a hill or hillock.

Barren could be the name for the site of Barry Island. Later on the name of the river that flows through the town came to be *Aberbarri* – a name which is recorded by John Leland in his book of travels, 1536-9.

This is the explanation you get from the late Melville Richards in *The Names of Towns and Cities in Britain*, and from other scholars. It's an explanation that depends on the belief that *Barren* was the earliest form of the name.

But what if the name was *Barri* from the beginning? It is worth remembering the name Barry Island – and Barry Island Farm! – near Porth-gain in Pembrokeshire. These could be Scandinavian names, going back to the time, 1000 years ago, when the Vikings were a trial and affliction to the inhabitants of the Welsh coasts.

Following this trail we might explain *Barri* as the name given by the Scandinavians to the island of Barri – this being a combination of the old Norse word *barr*, signifying a kind of barley, and the element *ey*, 'island', which we see in *Swansea* (Abertawe). As far as I can see, there is no way of settling the argument. Perhaps, indeed, it can never be settled conclusively.

An aerial photograph of Barry docks

BERMO and BERFFRO
(Barmouth and Aberffro)

The map says *Abermo*, we say *Y Bermo* in everyday speech
– yet the name of the river that flows into the sea there is
Mawddach. So the question is how to explain the apparent
confusion here.

Start with *Mawdd* – probably a personal name. Add
the ending *wy* to it – the *wy* that signals the name of a
tribe or the territory belonging to it, as in *Ardudwy* and
Deganwy. That gives you *Mawddwy*, the title of the
commote or district that was united with other districts to
create Meirionnydd by the Acts of Union, 1536 – 1542.

Mawdd was also the name of a river, and *Mawddach* (or
Mawdd bach, 'little Mawdd') that of one of its tributaries.
The place where the *Mawdd* river flowed into the sea
came to be called *Abermawdd*. In ordinary speech the *dd* at
the end was lost – just as, in the ordinary speech of
Pembrokeshire final *dd* is lost in such words as *gily(dd)*,
'other,' and *myny(dd)*, 'mountain,' 'hill'.

Abermawdd turned into *Abérmaw*, with the accent on
the *e*. In speech the name continued to evolve. The *aw*
changed to *o* in the same way as *dwylaw* ('hands')
changed to *dwylo*, and that gave *Abermo*. The initial *a* also
dropped off, although the trace of it that remains is the
cause of our invariable tendency to say '*Y Bermo*' rather
than – simply – 'Bermo'.

Look back at *Abermawdd* for a moment. It was the old
dd ending that caused the English to pronounce the name
as *Barmouth*. The fact is that the (English) word 'mouth' –

Welsh *ceg* – was never part of the name, which consists of *aber*, 'estuary', plus the name of the river – *Mawdd*.

In Anglesey we have the river *Ffraw*. Formerly the name of this was *Ffrawf* (meaning 'flood' or 'torrent') – which, etymologically, is the same as that of the rivers *Frome* in Dorset and Herefordshire respectively, the name itself being Welsh at root in each case.

The place where the river *Ffrawf* flowed into the sea was called *Aberffrawf*. The final *f* disappeared, *aw* changed to *o*, and the initial *a* was lost. Just as *Abermawdd* turned into *Abermo* and the latter into *Bermo*, so *Aberffrawf* became *Aberffro* and then *Berffro* – or very frequently *Y Berffro* in speech.

Nowadays the forms *Bermo* and *Berffro* are completely acceptable in Welsh.

The Mawddach estuary from the air

BETHLEHEM, EBENESER, DEINIOLEN

It's a very unexpected thing for visitors from a foreign country, seeing *Bethlehem* and *Nasareth* on names on road signs here in Wales.

Bethlehem is a village in the parish of Llangadog in Carmarthenshire. It's a small place – only a few houses, a post office and an Independent chapel. It's the post office which has made it famous during the course of recent years. Ever since special stamps began to be issued in celebration of Christmas, hundreds of people have been posting their Christmas cards in the village so as to get the *Bethlehem* postmark on them.

In the first place, of course, the village got its name from the Independent chapel, which was built there around 1820 and called *Bethlehem*. Later on the name of the chapel became the name for the village which grew up near it.

The same thing happened in the case of *Nasareth*, near Llanllyfni in Arfon. The Independent chapel there was built in 1823. In 1867, as the population increased following the growth of the slate industry, another chapel was built. This was called *Nasareth*, which also became the name for the houses around it.

In fact something similar occurred in many places in Wales. There's *Bethesda* in Dyffryn Ogwen, *Saron* near Rhydaman, *Nebo* near Llanrwst, and *Bethel*, *Carmel* and *Caesarea* outside Caernarfon. These Biblical names are as good an indication as any of the Nonconformist influence on everyday life in the new Wales that was coming into being in the first half of the nineteenthth century.

At one time *Ebeneser* was the name of a village above Dinorwig quarry, but that was changed by creating a new name from that of the parish of Llanddeiniolen. In his book *Hen Atgofion* ('Reminiscences'), W. J. Gruffydd has strong words to say about the change. The name Ebeneser, he says, arose naturally from the Nonconformist religion of the district, just as the parish name *Llanddeiniolen* (*llan* or church of St Deiniolen) arose from the religion of an earlier period. It is snobbery, says Gruffydd, to insist on resisting the simple dignity of Ebeneser. 'Deiniolen,' he comments in his incisive fashion, 'is a late fake seeking to imitate a genuine antique.'

Bethesda chapel

BETWS

There are two identical words *betws* in Welsh – but their meanings are very different.

One is an old homegrown term for a fairly steep slope or hillside where there is a thick growth of small hazel, thorn and birch trees – in fact the Welsh name *bedw*, for the birch tree, lies at the root of this term. Add the old plural ending – *os* to *bedw* and that gives you *bedwos*, a version of this being the name of a place – *Bedwas* – close to Caerffili (Caerphilly). You could translate that into English as 'birch grove.'

In speech *bedwos* became *betwos* in some districts, the *d* hardening to *t* in front of *w*, exactly as in *pysgotwr* (for *pysgodwr*), 'fisherman'. Later on the *o* in *betwos* was lost, to give *betws* as a term in parts of north-eastern and eastern Wales for a wooded slope. 'Mae y tir yn un betws,' they said there in the old days – that is, 'the ground is all over-run with underwood and small trees.'

Of purely English origin is the other word *betws*, the one that means 'church' as in the saying 'y byd a'r betws' ('the world and the church'). That comes from an old form for 'bead house' in English – the place where you went to pray. But 'necklace' is the meaning of 'beads' in English, some of you might say. Yes, certainly – nowadays. To begin with, however, the meaning of 'bead' was 'to pray'. The sense of 'necklace' came about because in the act of praying people used to count tiny balls on a string.*

The old church of St Michael's at Betws-y-coed

So a 'bead house' was a house into which one turned in order to say prayers, a small chapel or oratory as an adjunct to the parish church. The word itself was borrowed into Welsh as *betws* – the old form 'house' giving – *ws* or – *hws* (as with *becws*, 'bakehouse', and *warws*, 'warehouse'), and the *h* in *hws* hardening the *d* to *t*. Various old 'chapels of ease' bear the name *Betws* in Wales – *Betws Gwerful Goch* outside Corwen being one example.

One interesting thing about this name is that from it we learn that one *Gwerful* gave her name to the church.

Some of the genealogies make mention of Gwerful, daughter of Cynan ab Owain Gwynedd, adding that she was buried at Dinmael. King Owain Gwynedd died in 1170, and his son Cynan in 1174. That means that Gwerful flourished towards the year 1200 or a little before that. It appears that she encouraged the building of a chapel or small church and gave *Betws Gwerful Goch* its name.

* Hence the phrase 'telling their beads' – translator's note

BLAENYWEIRGLODD

This pleasing name is that of a farm in the vicinity of Llansannan (Denbighshire). But on the OS 'Landranger' map, 1986 edition, the name has been changed to *Blaen-y-wergloedd*. An unimportant change, you may think. No, not so. The change gives the official status of the OS map to an incorrect form, and that must be rejected.

Gweirglodd is the Welsh word for a piece of flat land – usually low-lying – where farmers used to grow grass for hay. The word is a combination of *gwair* (hay grass) and *clawdd* (dike, embankment) – *clawdd* because it was customary in former times to erect an embankment in order to enclose and protect the given piece of land, thus affording the grass a chance to grow. In fact the old Welsh laws specify the penalty that a pig owner had to pay if one of his pigs was caught rooting up the land 'within the *gweirglawdd* or meadow'.

The *aw* in the final unaccented syllable of *gweirglawdd* changed, giving *gweirglodd* – just as *Aberma*w(*dd*) changed to *Abérmo* (and *Bermo*) and *Aberffraw* to *Abérffro* (and *Berffro*). Also, in the spoken language *ei* in the first syllable came to be pronounced as *e* in northern Wales. And *y (g)weirglodd* became *y (g)werglodd* – just as the name *Gweirful* became *Gwerful*.

I'll accept *(g)werglodd* as a written version of the farm name if that was the acknowledged pronunciation in the district over the course of two or three generations. It's the *-oedd* at the end of the map-name that arouses my ire. There is only one reason for it – namely *via* someone thinking that *gwerglodd* is a plural name, and that the *-odd* at the end of it is a spoken version of the (plural) ending *-oedd*. But that is nonsense. *(G)wergloedd* is a fictitious form – the fruit of mistaken 'correction' stemming from ignorance. On the next edition of the 'Landranger' map *Blaenyweirglodd* ought to be restored – either that or the incorrect *spoken* form *Blaenywerglodd*.

In northern Wales *(g)werglodd* changed to give *(g)weirglodd* in speech. In southern Wales the change was different; there it became *gweirglod* (with the final *d* lost), and *gwerlod* or *gwrlod*. That's why you have farms and fields in Glamorgan and Monmouthshire with names such as *Gwrlodyfelin* and *Gwrlod-y-pownd*.*

The same word explains the name *Gwrlodde* to the south of Talgarth in Breconshire: this representing *gwrloddau*, a local variation of *gweirgloddiau* ('meadows').

* 'Meadow of the mill' and 'meadow of the pound' respectively – translator's note

BRAINT

Braint is the name of a river which rises in the Llwydiarth hills in Anglesey and falls into the sea at Traeth Melynog, opposite Caernarfon.

On the outskirts of London is the river *Brent*, one of the Thames tributaries; this river gave its name to the town *Brentford* because there was a ford across it at that point.

At root the two names are identical – *Braint* in Anglesey and *Brent* in London. Both go back to the name of the goddess Brigantia or Briganti in Brythonic, the language that gave rise to Welsh.

In the pre-Christian era, Brigantia was one of the goddesses of the Britons. The river in the London area and the one in Anglesey were named after her by speakers of Brythonic who sought her patronage and protection. That was 2000 years ago or thereabouts: place-names are capable of carrying echoes or resonances of this sort which go back to the very distant past.

But – some of you may say – the common Welsh word *braint* implies special honour or status. Yes, certainly, and that is also part of the story. *Braint* – which was something like *brigant* in its old Brythonic form – denoted a free man, one having rights and social standing. That explains how the tribe of the *Brigantes* got their name. They looked on themselves as privileged ones, a unique people.

Their special region was the part of the country that corresponds today to the north of England. There they were the leading lights in some sort of federation of small territories stretching from Elfed (around Leeds) to the south of Scotland. Brigantia was their goddess. But reverence for her extended beyond the kingdom of the Brigantes themselves. Britons of other tribes and territories – as in Anglesey and the London area – acknowledged her and bestowed her name on rivers.

BRANDY BACH

Those oral verses of an earlier time which listed place-names are amusing things. This one from north-eastern Wales, for example:

> *Wrecsam Fechan a Wrecsam Fawr,*
> *Pentrefelin ac Adwy'r Clawdd,*
> *Casgen Ditw a Thafarn-y-Gath,*
> *Llety Llygoden a Brandy Bach.*

> (Little Wrexham and Big Wrexham,
> Mill Village and Gap-in-the-Dyke,
> Pussy's Barrel and the Cat's Inn,
> Mouse's Lodging and Little *Brandy*.)

The rhymes or half-rhymes – *mawr/clawdd; cath/bach* – demonstrate to perfection the oral pedigree of the verse, with the last two lines including the names of four inns in the Llandegla area (in Denbighshire).

Cat's Inn is the best-known of them. A sort of meeting of poets, dubbed the 'Eisteddfod in the Cat's Inn', was held in 1719. And then, in the nineteenth century, William Jones, the 'Lark of the Hill Country', lived there for a while as a discontented publican.

Brandy Bach, now. What do you make of the name? Before rushing to conclude that here we have the English word 'brandy', consider this: there used to be a word *ebran* in Welsh meaning 'provender for animals' – and, in particular, provender for horses. The word occurs in the

39

old version of the Bible. There, in Isaiah, chapter 30 (verse 24), there is a reference to oxen and asses, stating that they 'shall eat' *ebran pur* – 'clean provender'.

Add the word tŷ ('house') to *ebran* – just as you add *tŷ* to *bwyd* ('food') or to *llaeth* ('milk') so as to get *bwyty* ('restaurant') and *llaethdy* ('dairy'). And there you have *ebrandy*, which became *brandy* colloquially, a word for a house where provender for horses was available. It's very possible that there was a *Brandy Bach* in Llandegla – an inn where it was customary for travellers to stop in order to take liquid refreshment on their own account and in order for the horses to get rest and provender.

I wonder whether the same thing applied to *Brandy Bach* in Dolbenmaen in Eifionydd and *Brandy* in Mallwyd (Meirionnydd). It's an interesting possibility.

BROGYNTYN

This is the name of a mansion in the parish of Selatyn, near Croesoswallt (Oswestry) in Shropshire. *'Brogyntyn, or Porkington* as it was anglicised in the Tudor period,' says the *Companion to Welsh Literature* when discussing it. But I wonder, I wonder: is this really a Welsh name that acquired an English guise?

It appears in the year 1161 as *Porchington* and in 1236 as *Porkington* in civil records – that is, as an English name.

The simple way to explain Porkington is to assume that it is one of those English place-names that contain a personal name at the beginning, then the element *ing* meaning 'connected with that person,' and – added on the end afterwards – the word *tūn* meaning 'estate' or 'settlement.'

A good example of the type is *Paddington*, the name of the station in London. It denotes an estate which, in the early period when the place was named, was connected with someone called *Padda*.

Porkington, or *Porkingtun* in its old form, was an estate or settlement connected with *Porca* – this possibly being the by-name or nickname of some early Englishman in the locality. That is the explanation you are given by that great place-name scholar Eilert Ekwall in his *Oxford Dictionary of English Place-Names*.

But the inhabitants of *Porkingtun* in the Middle Ages were Welsh-speaking Welsh people, and it was by them that the name was 'cymricised'. The *tūn* on the end became *tyn* – as in *Prestatyn*, from the Old English *Prēosta-*

tūn, 'farm or estate of the priests.' In addition the *k* was softened to *g*, giving the spoken form *Porgintyn*. This changed to *Borgintyn* and *Borgyntyn* – a form which is recorded for it. Then *Borgyntyn* changed yet again in speech to *Brogyntyn*. And since *bro* is a common Welsh word, it was naturally assumed that this was an original part of the name.

The English place-name *Porkington*, which was 'cymricised' to *Brogyntyn*, is the name of Lord Harlech's residence, and it is testimony to how strongly and tenaciously the Welsh language has stood its ground through many centuries in the Oswestry region.

CAERDYDD
(Cardiff)

Caerdydd is the (Welsh) name of the capital of Wales.

It would be very easy to think that *Caerdydd* is the combination of *caer*, 'fort', and the Welsh word *dydd* ('day'). This would be a great mistake, and an example of seeking to explain a place-name on the basis of its form as it is today, without looking to see what the old form was.

It's true that *Caerdydd* has been the name for a span of 200 years. But before that it was *Caerdyf*. An old Welsh poet speaks of going

'To Caerdyf and the tavern'.

Our task, then, is to explain the form *Caerdyf*.

Let us take the name *Caergybi*, the Welsh name for Holyhead. *Caergybi* was formed from *caer* and the name of the saint *Cybi* – the *c* in Cybi being lenited to *g* at the beginning of the second element of a compound word, according to the custom in Welsh. In *Caerdyf*, *caer* must have been followed by an original form Tyf.* But what is *Tyf*?

The river that flows through the capital is called the *Taf*. The old genitival form of this was *Tyf*. The meaning of *Caerdyf*, then, was *caer yr afon Taf* – 'fort of the river Taf'.

In spoken Welsh *Caerdyf* changed to *Caerdydd* – the *f* (or *v*) changing to *dd*. In English, *Caerdyf* was preserved, but with the Welsh *f* (or *v*) being pronounced as an English *f* and written as *ff*.

Llandaf is the name of the cathedral church, 'the *llan* (church) on the river Taf.' Llandaf is an exceedingly old name. But *Caerdyf* must be older still. If it contains the genitival form *Tyf*, it must go back to a very early period of the Welsh language – perhaps to the sixth century.

* I. e. with lenition of *t* to *d* – translator's note

The Millennium Stadium at Cardiff

CAERFYRDDIN
(Carmarthen)

The earliest written evidence we possess for place-names in Wales consists of forms recorded by some of the Greek and Roman authors of the ancient world.

There is the mathematician and astronomer of Alexandria, Claudius Ptolemaeus or Ptolemy. Somewhere around 150 AD he wrote a treatise in Greek, the *Geography*. In it are references to places in Britain – to *Maridunum*, for example.

Maridunum, with *a* in the first syllable, is in Ptolemy's treatise. But scholars who specialise in these matters agree that the *a* is an error for *o*, and that *Moridunum* is the correct name.

Moridunum: that was the name in Brythonic, i.e. the kind of Celtic language that was spoken in Britain 2000 years ago, and the language from which Welsh sprang *via* natural processes.

Let's dwell for a moment on the form *Moridunum*. We can divide it into two words – *mori* and *dunum*. Take the second one, *dunum*. We can forget the ending *-um*. That leaves the stem *dun*, a word meaning 'fort'. In Welsh this changed to *din* – the same *din* as in *dinas* ('city'). Then *mori*. Forget the ending *-i*, which leaves *mor* – an early form of our *môr*, 'sea'.

Moridunum was a combination of words meaning 'sea' and 'fort' respectively. Its meaning was 'fort by the sea', or 'sea fort'.

As Brythonic changed slowly into Welsh, *Moridunum*

Coracles on the river Tywi, Carmarthen

became *Myrddin*. And at one period in the history of the Welsh language *Myrddin* was the name of the place which was known as *Moridunum* in the time of Ptolemy.

Later on the fact that the name *Myrddin* already contained within it the word *din* meaning 'fort' was overlooked. So the word *caer* was added to it – unnecessarily – and that brought the name *Caerfyrddin* into existence.

Other names, like *Caergybi* (Holyhead) and *Caer-gai* were a combination of *caer* and a personal name – here Cybi, Cai. It came to be thought that Caerfyrddin was similar – a combination of *caer* with the personal name *Myrddin*.* And traditions about the ancient bard and magician of the name Myrddin were linked – quite groundlessly – with the town.

But Myrddin's – or Merlin's – is another story, one which it would take a whole book to trace.

* With *m* lenited to *f* – translator's note

One of the coraclemen of Carmarthen

CAERNARFON

In the tale about Branwen in the *Mabinogi*, Branwen sends a starling from Ireland to Wales to tell Brân the Blessed, her elder brother, how the Irish are mistreating and punishing her. The starling safely crosses the sea and finds its way to Brân in the midst of his counsellors – and all this, in the words of the tale, in 'Caer Seint in Arfon'.

This was the name of Caernarfon at the time when the tale of Branwen was written – which, of course, was before the building of the great Norman castle we're familiar with on the quay.

The old fort, pre-dating Edward's castle, was the Roman one on the hill near Llanbeblig church – *Segontium* to you and me today, but *Caer Saint* (or *Caer Seint*) to our ancestors.

Yes, to the Romans it was *Segontium*. When they first came to Eryri (Snowdonia), they adopted the name of the river in the Brythonic tongue as that of the fort built by them. That name was *Segonti*, containing the root *seg* and meaning – perhaps – 'flowing strongly'. It's the same root *seg* which is at the beginning of Siguenza, the name of a Spanish town between Madrid and Zarogoza.

In the course of time, as Brythonic changed into Welsh, so *Segonti* changed into *Seint* (or *Saint*). The Welsh called the Roman fort *Caer Seint yn Arfon* and the mouth of the river, where Edward's castle was built, *Aber-seint* – or possibly *Aber-sein* in everyday speech.

Caer Seint yn Arfon was a mouthful of a name; the next natural step was its contraction. It became *Caer yn Arfon*

The imperial castle on the banks of Seiont and Menai

and, in the spoken language, the single word *Caernarfon* – which, by now, has been contracted again to *Cnarfon*.

For historians of the language there is one problem in

connexion with this explanation. Usually an *s* at the beginning of a Brythonic word gives *h* in Welsh. The river called *Sabrina* in Brythonic gave the name *Severn* in English, with the *s* remaining. In Welsh, in accordance with the regular characteristics of the language, the name changed to *Hafren*.

From *Segonti*, according to this usual pattern, one might have expected *Haint* to be the name of the river. But *Saint* it is. Why the difference? One possible answer is that a form like *Segonti* was part of the everyday speech of Latin-speaking people in Caernarfon long enough for the initial *s* to be retained.

Thus far I have referred without exception to the river *Saint*, and not to the *Seiont*. The fact is that *Seiont* is a 'learned' artificial form based on *Segontium*.

CASNEWYDD
(Newport)

The earliest form we have for the name of this town in Monmouthshire is *Novus Burgus* in a document of the year 1138. This is a Latin form, of course, comprising *novus*, 'new', and a Latinisation of the Old English word *burh* meaning 'town'.

Behind the *Novus Burgus* of the document was the English name *Newburh*, namely the 'new town' that was built by the Normans. The same elements *new* and *burh* gave Newbury in Berkshire its name; that was also a new town built in the time of the Normans.

In the case of the Monmouthshire town the second element *burh* was supplanted fairly early on by the word *port*, to give Newport. 'Town' or 'market town' was the meaning of *port* here, exactly as in the Newport on the Isle of Wight, and in the second part of Stockport.

The Welsh name was Castell Newydd ar Wysg ('new castle on the Usk'). That's how you find it spelt 600 years ago. In everyday speech *Castell* at the beginning was abbreviated to *Cas*. Castell Newydd became *Casnewydd*, just as Castell Gwent became *Cas-gwent*, Castell Llwchwr *Casllwchwr*, and the Pembrokeshire Castell Mael *Cas-mael*.

Newport is also the English name for the Pembrokeshire Trefdraeth. It's hard to be sure what *port* signifies in this name. It could mean 'town' or 'market town'. It could also have the sense 'harbour', as in Portsmouth. In the case of Newport in Monmouthshire there's scarcely any doubt. The old forms of the name show that *port* in the sense of 'town', 'market town' is what we have here.

Newport docks

CASTELL-NEDD
(Neath)

It was a river that gave its name to the town *Castell-nedd*, as in the case of Cardiff. And just as with Cardiff, the name of the river is extremely old – in this case going back 2,000 years. For this we have the testimony of the Romans.

The Roman custom was to draw up lists of the imperial roads – early versions of gazetteers, naming town and forts and noting the number of miles between them. One of these gazetteers is the *Itinerarium... Antonini*, or *Antonine Itinerary*, which was probably drawn up somewhere between 200 and 300 AD.

One of the routes in this Itinerary is that from Viroconium – Wroxeter near Shrewsbury – down to *Caerllion* (Caerleon) and across to Carmarthen. On the route there is a reference to *Nido* (or *Nidum*).

This was the Romans' name for their fort on the banks of the river *Nida*. And *Nida*? That was what the river was called by the local inhabitants in Brythonic, the language from which Welsh sprang. In time, as Brythonic developed into Welsh, *Nida* changed to *Nedd*; the final *a* was lost, but left its mark on the *i*, turning it into *e*, while the *d* between two consonants was lenited to *dd*.

But what was the meaning of *Nedd* or *Nida*? No one knows for certain. It's possible that it was a Celtic word meaning 'bright', 'shining'.

A little later than the Roman period a castle was built on the bank of the river Nedd, and the Welsh came to call the town that grew up around it *Castell-nedd*. The Normans and the English had difficulty in pronouncing *Nedd*, and forms such as *Neth*, *Neeth* and *Neath* which occur in documents reflect their attempts to write the Welsh name.

Neath castle

CICHLE

Cichle is the name of a farm in the village of Llan-faes near Beaumaris, in Anglesey. The name also occurs in Llandegfan, *Allt Cichle* being the name of a steep hill rising from the Beaumaris road at Llandegfan soon after you leave Porthaethwy (Menai Bridge). Where the hill is today, there was once land called *Cae Cichle* or *Tyddyn Cichle*.

At first glance *Cichle* looks like a good Welsh name. The *-ch-* in the middle and the *-le* (*lle*, 'place') at the end give that impression. But in fact its Welsh appearance is totally misleading.

The truth of it is that Cichle is a foreign name. To explain it we have to go back nearly 600 years, and to the town of Beaumaris around the time of Owain Glyndŵr. One of the Englishmen who came to the town at that time was *John Kyghley, knight*, who probably hailed from Keighley in Yorkshire.

Today we *might* be pronouncing the name of this man, and the name of the West Riding town where his family originated, as *Kiffli**. But in former times the letters *gh* did not have the sound *ff* in English; they were pronounced much more like our *ch*.

In the dictionary he compiled in order to help Welsh people master English, the Welshman William Salesbury says (1547) that *gh* is 'the same sound as our *ch*', but that in English it is pronounced less gutturally than the North Welsh *ch*.

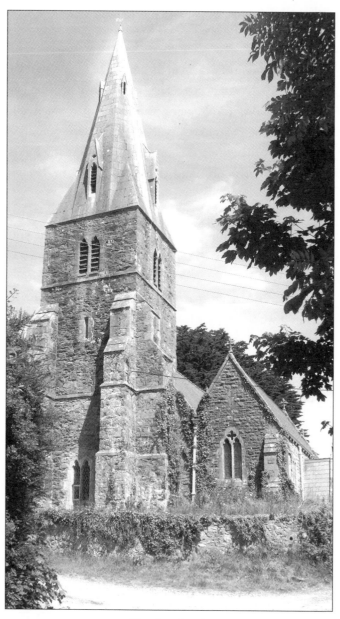

Llan-faes church

Nowadays one says *draught* for beer straight out of the cask, while pronouncing it *drafft*. At one time the English word was closer in its sound to *dracht*, and from that we get *dracht* ('draught of beer' etc.) and *drachtio* ('to drink deep') in Welsh. In the same way the sound *ch* was 'hard' in English in the name John Kyghley, but to the Welsh people living in the locality of Beaumaris around 1411 he was John *Cichli* or John *Cichlei*. In 1415 this John Cichlei took possession of land in the vicinity of Beaumaris that had belonged to the Crown. In course of time the land came to be called 'Land of *Cichlei*', then *Cichle*.

So that is *Cichle*: the family name of English people from Keighley who held land in the region almost 600 years ago. The name preserves a memory of past regional history – and of English speech when the (guttural-sounding) *ch* existed in that language.

* I.e. by analogy with the pronunciation of *-gh* in English words like 'rough', 'tough' etc. – translator's note

CORWEN

There is a temptation to look at the name *Corwen* in Denbighshire and to see the adjective *gwen* (feminine form of *gwyn*), 'white' as the second element in it. But to follow that trail would be entirely wrong.

All the earliest written forms are in agreement that the name used to be *Corfaen* (*Corvaen* in ecclesiastical documents of 1254 and 1291, for example, *Corvayn* in 1309). Thus the second element is *maen* * – the same *maen* as in *Maentwrog*, stone commemorating Saint Twrog.

In Welsh, *f* and *w* in the middle of a word can sometimes interchange. Where I refer to a *cawod* ('shower') of rain, others refer to a *cafod*. Similarly, *Corfaen* changed to *Corwaen*, and at the same time the *ae* in the last

A Telford milestone on the A5

Corwen bridge

unaccented syllable changed to *e*. By around 1400, *Corwen* was both the spoken and written form. What about the *cor* at the beginning of it? *Cor* can mean 'small', as in *corrach*, 'dwarf', 'small man'. So *Corfaen* could signify 'small stone' – compare *corbys*, 'small pea'. In the Book of Ezekiel in the Bible there is a reference to the making of bread with 'wheat and barley and beans and chickpeas and millet and *corbys* – 'lentils' in the English Bible.

But there are other meanings of *cor* or *côr*. It can signify the chancel or sanctuary of a church, as well as the part of a cowshed or stable where animals are tethered. The ecclesiastical meaning would fit exactly in the case of *Corfaen* or *Corwen*, as in that of *Maentwrog*. A stone marking a consecrated spot – that would be the *corfaen* that gave the place its name to begin with.

* With *m* lenited to *f/v* – translator's note

59

CRICIETH

Crukeith, spelt like that, is the earliest form I've seen for the name *Cricieth*. It was recorded in 1273 or 1274, before Edward I built the Norman castle there.

Note that *u*, and not *i*, was the vowel in the first part. That tells us that the word *crug*, meaning 'hillock', was the first element of the name – the same *crug* as in Crucywel (Crickhowell), Crucadarn, and the last part of Yr Wyddgrug (Mold).

The second element was *ceith* or *caith* –– a plural of *caeth* and signifying 'bondmen' in English – either those who were tenants in bondage to the land and without rights, or possibly actual prison inmates. The *Chronicle of the Princes* tells us that Dafydd ap (*'son of'*) Llywelyn Fawr ('the Great') imprisoned his brother 'in Cruceith': so the hillock or tump was the site of a prison.

In time *Cruceith* became *Crucieith*, with an *i* developing in speech after the *c* – as in *ciapten* for *capten* ('captain'). Later on *Crucieith* became *Cricieith* – the *u* changing to *i* under the influence of the *i* sound that follows it. And then, by 1600, *Cricieith* became *Cricieth*.

In the case of *Cricieth*, the evidence of forms in old records makes it easy for us to trace how the name changed. But how to spell it? How many *c*'s ought there to be in the middle? I've written one *c* in this article, but some good people of the town say there ought to be two.

The truth is that down the centuries there have been around forty different ways of spelling the name. You find *c* and *k* for the initial *c*; *c*, *kk*, *cc*, *ck* and even *kk* for the *c* in the middle; *t* as well as *th* for the *th* on the end; and other variations to denote the vowels.

This is not at all strange. Clerks, many of them foreign, had difficulty through the centuries in writing down Welsh names. And the standardisation of Welsh orthography was a comparatively late thing – i.e. the settling on an agreed standard way of spelling. That was brought about by Sir John Morris-Jones and his co-scholars around the beginning of the nineteenth century. It was agreed to write a single *c* and a single *m* at all times, even if – in strict phonetic terms – one or other of them was a double consonant. Thus it is *Cricieth* with one *c* which is correct. There's no arguing about that. The desire to write *Criccieth* is a whim, and nothing else.

Cricieth castle on its hillock above the old town

CROESCWRLWYS
(Culverhouse Cross)

Croescwrlwys – or *Culverhouse Cross* in English – is where the ITV Wales & West studio is located on the outskirts of Cardiff, in the direction of Y Barri (Barry).

It's easy to explain the *Croes* and the *Cross* in the respective namings. This is the place where the old Cardiff to Pen-y-bont road crossed the one from Y Barri to Sain Ffagan (St Fagans). It used to be a crossroad of importance.

In Glamorgan the old word for a crossroad or crossway was *croesheol* or *croesewl*. The form *Croesheol* for the crossroad in question occurs on an old map of around 1762-3, and the English *Crossway* in documents earlier than that. Nearby was a farm called *Culverhouse*. The name of the farm was attached to that of the *croesewl* to give *Culverhouse Cross* – the name of our crossroad.

What about *Culverhouse*? Today the name strikes us as unfamiliar, but go back a few hundred years and *culver* was a common English word for a dove or pigeon; in parts of southern England it still survives as a word for the wood-pigeon.

In days gone by also, *culverhouse* was a common word for a dovecot. That takes us back to the time when pigeons were part of the menu at banquets, and when lords of the manor and monks reared the birds in dovecots.

In spoken Welsh the name of the farm, *Culverhouse*, was corrupted to *Cwrlws* and *Cwrlwys*. Thus *Croescwrlwys* is the name for a crossroad near a farm called *Culverhouse* where there was once a dovecot.

CRUCYWEL
(Crickhowell)

I have seen the name *Crucywel* explained as *Crug-yr-awel*, but that explanation is completely without foundation.

The earliest available forms – *Crickhoel* in 1263, *Crukhowell* in 1281 – tell their story clearly enough. They are a combination of the common noun *crug* and the personal name *Hywel* after it. In old medieval documents you see Hywel frequently spelt as *Hoel* and *Hoell*.

The meaning of *crug* is quite clear. It can denote a hillock or tump, while – in the form *cricin* – it can be used for a mass: the expression *cricin o bobl* is one heard in southern Wales for a *mass* of people. It can also denote a cairn or mound (*carnedd*), and occurs frequently in this sense as the term for a hillock where there are prehistoric remains.

In the case of *Crug Hywel*, the initial *h* of *Hywel* has caused the hardening of the final *g* of *crug* to give *Cruc Hywel* or *Crucywel*. Similar hardening occurs when a word beginning with *c* comes after *crug*. *Crug Cadarn*, for example: that becomes *Crucadarn*, the name of another place in Breconshire. But there is no reason whatsoever for spelling these names as *crick-!*

Incidentally, it's the Welsh (or Brythonic) word *crug* which is found in the village name *Crich* near Derby, and in the second part of *Penkridge* between Stafford and Wolverhampton. At root, Penkridge represents *Pen-crug*.

CWM-BRÂN

Cwm-brân is the youngest town in Wales. It was built in the 1950s, in the wake of the New Towns Law, as a home for workers in the industries that were growing up between Newport and Pontypool.

The name itself existed earlier – as that of a village and previously that of a farm – in the valley (*cwm*) of a small river or brook called Brân which flowed down westwards to join the river Llwyd. But the new town is a little below the old Cwm Brân. It was therefore the river or brook called Brân that gave the new town its name. But why call a river *Brân*?

After *brân* ('raven', 'crow'), some people think – because the water of the river is black. True, perhaps. But naming rivers after birds is not a common practice in Wales, as far as my observation extends.

Others reckon what we have here is the personal name *Brân*. That's possible. But one fact requires notice: *Brân* occurs several times as the name of brooks, especially in southern Wales.

There's the Brân that flows into the Arth near Cross Inn in Ceredigion; another Brân that joins the Tywi (Towy) in Llandovery, and yet another in the region of Glansefin, to the east of Llangadog. And there are several others besides these. Add too the Brenig in Tregaron and the Brenig on Mynydd Hiraethog in Denbighshire (*Brân*, that is, plus the diminutive termination -*ig*: 'little Brân' is the meaning of these last two.)

Why is *Brân* so common a name for brooks or fairly

small rivers – including the one after which the town Cwm-brân was named? There must be some simple explanation, if only we were able to hit on it.

CWM-Y-GLO

Why, you may wonder, is there a village of the name *Cwm-y-glo* ('valley of coal') between Llanberis and Caernarfon, in a place where there has never been a coal pit in its vicinity? The answer is that *glo* in Welsh can mean 'charcoal' (also 'coke') as well as the usual 'coal'. Charcoal (*golosg*) is the meaning of the *glo* in *Cwm-y-glo*. It used to be the custom at one time there to burn wood in order to produce charcoal.

The preparation of charcoal was an important craft in former times, and one requiring considerable skill. Wood had to be cut into lengths of a particular size, and then carefully packed so as to ensure that it would burn slowly – smoulder into charcoal, and not burst into flame.

Another name which preserves the memory of this old custom is *Gloddaith*, near Llandudno – that of a house which was the home of the Mostyn family. The word *Gloddaith* is a combination of *glo* and the element *daith* which is in the word *goddaith*, whose meaning is 'large fire', 'bonfire'. It is also the term for the burning of gorse, heather and ferns at the beginning of Spring.

Gloddaith was the name of a location where wood was burned to produce charcoal. When you consider that the name occurs in a record of 1298, that tells us that the preparation of charcoal was a craft in existence in the Llandudno area before that year – and probably a good time before it.

Gloddaith, near Llandudno, once the home of the Mostyn family

Another form for *golosg* was *golosged*. That word still survives in south-western Wales for stumps of burnt gorse, and it explains the name Losged, denoting a piece of common land near Cwmcamlais in Breconshire.

CYDWELI
(Kidwelly)

The English antiquary John Leland, who lived around 450 years ago, was the first to try to explain the name *Cydweli*. He mentions a *Kidwely* or *Cathgweli*, and then assumes that *gwely* ('bed') is the second part of the name and *cath* ('cat') the first. According to him, some special cat made its bed in an oak tree here. The place was called *Cathgwely*, which soon became *Cedwely* and *Cidwely*.

Leland is completely wide of the mark, you might say. Yes indeed. But equally without foundation is another popular explanation one is always hearing, namely that the combination in question is *cyd* ('shared') and *gwely*, since the town lies between the *bed* of the river Gwendraeth Fawr and that of the Gwendraeth Fach. The plain truth is that the name has nothing whatsoever to do with a bed of any kind.

Cetgueli, spelt like that, is the earliest available form of the name. It's an old form, recorded more than a thousand years ago. At that time the name itself denoted a commote, or piece of land. And the fact that it did so is important for the explanation of it. What we have here is a personal name, *Cadwal*, and the termination *-i* that was sometimes added to a person's name in order to designate his land.

The *-i* caused the two *a*'s in *Cadwal* to mutate to *e*: that is, *Cadwal* + *i* became *Cedweli* – the meaning of which would be 'land belonging to Cadwal and his descendants.'

The name *Ceri* – denoting a commote or portion of

land in Montgomeryshire – is of the same type. Originally it designated the land of someone called *Car*. When *-i* was added to *Car*, it changed naturally to *Ceri*.

Names like these, where the *-i* ending has been added to the name of a person to give that of a portion of land, are extremely old, dating back to a very early period in the history of the Welsh language.

At the outset, then, *Cedweli* – or *Cetgueli* according to old way of spelling – denoted a piece of land. Later on, after the building of the Norman castle, it became the name of the Carmarthenshire town.

Cedweli, with *e* following the *c*, is the traditional and correct form of the name. In everyday speech we tend to pronounce it *Cydweli*, and because that form has also been *written* for more than 500 years, custom is reason enough for keeping it.

An aerial photograph of Kidwelly castle on the bank of Gwendraeth Fach

CYNCOED

Cyncoed is the name of a part of Cardiff. So what about it?

The simple answer is that the original name was *Cefncoed* or *Cefn-coed* ('ridge of the wood'). In a document of 1703, which was printed in the 1883 number of the periodical *Archaeologia Cambrensis*, the name appears in the forms *Kevencoyd* and *Hewl* y Keven-coyd*.

Kevencoyd – i.e. *Cefen-coed* – is an interesting form. It shows the word becoming *cefen* in the spoken tongue when uttered on its own. In the dialects of southern Wales a vowel develops between *f* and *n* at the end of a monosyllabic word. A North Walian says *ofn* ('fear') and *cafn* ('trough'); in the south one hears *ofon* and *cafan*. A northerner says *cefn*, a southerner *cefen*.

When *f* and *n* are bunched together (*fn*) at the end of the first part of a disyllable, there is a tendency in the south for the *f* to be lost. *Cefnder* is the word for a male cousin; this is the northern pronunciation, while in the south one hears *cender*. In the same way you hear *cenffordd* in the south for *cefnffordd* ('ridgeway') – as in the place-name *Penygenffordd* near Talgarth in Breconshire.

On the same pattern as *cender* and *cenffordd* for *cefnder* and *cefnffordd*, so *cefncoed* – a strict compound – could become *cencoed* in southern Wales. That's what occurred in the case of *Cefncoed* in Cardiff: colloquially, it became *Cencoed*, and there is evidence for that in old documents. Later on the *cen* part changed once more, to *cyn*, giving the form *Cyncoed*.

We can now re-create the story of the name. First there was *Cefn-coed*, then *Cefncoed*, later on *Cencoed*, and later still *Cyncoed*.

These forms are a good example of how a language changes across the centuries in its spoken form. It's proof also that there is no such thing in a living language as forms which are 'correct' forever. After all, no one today would be looking to restore the old form *Cefncoed* in place of *Cyncoed*.

* 'Road', 'way' – translator's note

CHWITFFORDD
(Whitford)

What do you make of Chwitffordd? That is the usual form in Welsh for the name of a village in Flintshire, between Prestatyn and Treffynnon, which was the home of Thomas Pennant (1726-98).*

The name in English is *Whitford* – a very old name. It occurs in the form *Widford* in Domesday Book, the famous survey of the lands in his kingdom which was made at the command of William the Conqueror in 1086. The name is a combination of *ford* (Welsh *rhyd*) – i.e. for crossing a river – and an old form of *wide* or *white*. It describes either a wide ford or one where either the water or the river-bed was white in appearance.

Of course, *Widford* or *Whitford* is older than Domesday Book. It's one of the Old English names which testify to the possession by the English of parts of north-east Wales as early as the eighth century – more than 1200 years ago.

What about the Welsh name for the village? *Chwitffordd* is the usual form – the one in the University of Wales *Gazetteer of Place-names* and on the Welsh map of Wales published in 1991 by Estate Publications in Newtown. But some Welsh people in Flintshire object to *Chwitffordd* and are seeking to replace it with *Rhydwen* or *Rhyd-wen*.

I would not pour cold water on the 'cymricising' zeal of those people who are pushing *Rhydwen*. But in the matter of this particular name I disagree with them.

There are a score or more places called *Rhydwen* or

Rhyd-wen in Wales. In Anglesey there is one where Rhyd-wen has changed to Rhyd-wyn. But there is no evidence that Rhydwen is an old name in the region in question. In fact the late Ellis Davies, writing in the periodical *Archaeologia Cambrensis* in 1921, clearly states that Rhydwen is a very recent form there. (Incidentally, it was this comparatively late Rhydwen in Flintshire that gave its name to the poet Rhydwen Williams; his father came from this region.)

On the other hand, Chwitffordd is old. It occurs in the form Chwitforth in a letter written by the rector of the parish on 3 November 1284 to acknowledge that he has received compensation of 13 shillings for the damage done to the church during the attacks of the English king against Llywelyn.

So it was Chwitffordd in 1284 and surely long before that. The form with *chw* at the beginning and *dd* at the end is proof that Welsh people in the region had 'cymricised' the English Whitford at a very early period.

And Chwitffordd – like Prestatyn in place of Preston – testifies to the fact that Welsh was regaining ground in north-east Wales some 900 years ago. The form is a small but important part of our history and heritage.

* Welsh naturalist and antiquary – translator's note

DISERTH or DYSERTH

Dyserth is a village in Flintshire, between Rhuddlan and Prestatyn. *Diserth* is the name of a parish in Radnorshire, a little to the north of Llanfair-ym-Muallt (Builth Wells). And – according to the OS map – there's a farm called *Dyserth* just to the south of Y Trallwng (Welshpool).

You'd be surprised, I'm sure, if someone told you there was a close relationship between these three place-names and the English word *desert* meaning 'waste', 'wilderness'. But that's the truth of it.

The *Dyserth* in Flintshire, the *Diserth* in Radnorshire, and the *Dyserth* near Y Trallwng: all three names are forms of an old Welsh word *diserth*. In strictly correct terms, Diserth – with an *i* – ought to be the form of the place-name in each instance.

And the old word *diserth* itself? To explain that we are obliged to start with the Latin *desertus*, signifying a desolate and uninhabited location. *Desert* in English is a borrowing of the Latin word.

In the Latin of the Early Church, *desertum* – or *disertum* in speech – came to denote the sort of wild and isolated place to which religious men used to retreat in order to live as hermits. The Welsh word *diserth* was borrowed from the *disertum* of ecclesiastical Latin; it signified a hermit's cell, the sort of place where certain of the old 'saints' retreated from the world.

In each of the three places in Wales mentioned above

there was once, long ago, the refuge or retreat of some holy man or other.

In Ireland you often find *Disert* and *Desart* in place-names. These also represent borrowings from ecclesiastical Latin, and each preserves the memory of some hermit's retreat.

ESGOBAETH BRÂN

This is the name of a farmstead in central Anglesey, between Llangefni and Pentraeth. At first glance the name looks dignified enough – until you start to think about it. Then questions arise.

Why call a farm in the middle of the countryside a 'bishopric' (*esgobaeth*)? And who or what is the *brân* in the name – the bird ('crow'), or the Brân of whom it is related in the *Mabinogi* that he crossed the sea to Ireland to redress the wrong done to his sister? And what has either a carrion-crow or a pre-Christian demi-god to do with a bishopric? By the time you've asked these questions it's clear that the name *Esgobaeth Brân* is pretty odd to say the least.

It was Professor Melville Richards, one of the great pioneers of Welsh place-name study, who explained the oddity. Searching among old papers of the Penrhyn estate he noticed that 500 years ago the name was *Tyddyn Gobaith Brân*, 'crow's-hope smallholding' – that is, a smallholding on which only a crow could hope to subsist.

At the outset the name was satirical, a kind of nickname. Later on, in everyday speech, the initial word *tyddyn* was lost, leaving only *Gobaith Brân*. The next step was that someone, around 1780, assumed that the latter name was a corruption of *Esgobaeth Brân*. A new and fictitious form was created. This was recorded on the first Ordnance map of 1838 and on every map subsequently.

Incidentally, you find examples of farmsteads in England called 'Crow Comfort Farm' – which, not infrequently, gets changed to 'Cold Comfort Farm'.

GABALFA

When I was a child and had eaten a hearty meal, my Nain (Welsh for 'grandmother') used to ask playfully, 'Did you get your *ceubal-ful*?' In Nain's everyday parlance, *llond dy geubal* was an affectionate was of saying 'your bellyful'.

Used figuratively or metaphorically, *ceubal* can mean 'belly' or 'stomach'. But its literal meaning in Welsh was 'boat', and more particularly 'flat-bottomed boat for crossing a river' – i.e. 'ferry'. In the old Welsh law-books, where the prices of various implements are mentioned, a coracle worth eight pence is listed along with a *ceubal* worth twenty-four pence.

It's customary in Welsh to add *-ma* or *-fa* (with *m* lenited to *f*) to the ends of words denoting places with special significance. Add *-ma* to *glan* and that yields *glanfa*, 'landing-place', 'quay'. Add *-ma* to *ceubal* and that gives *ceubalfa* as the word for a place where there was a *ceubal* or boat for crossing a river. Put the definite article in front of it and you have *Y Geubalfa*, which in speech became *Y Gabalfa* and *Gabalfa* (with *c* lenited to *g*).

The name *Gabalfa* survives in Cardiff for a place where at one time a *ceubal* used to offer a ferry service across the river Taf. There's another *Cabalfa* on the river Wye between Rhydspence and Clyro: a farm, Upper Cabalfa, which merely preserves the name today but where, in former times, there was also a ferry for crossing the river.

Another word for a small flat-bottomed boat was *cafn*, 'trough' – probably because it was hollowed out from a solid piece of wood. There was a boat of this sort at Cafn

Gronant in Dyffryn Conwy, where Tal-y-*cafn* stands today. It's interesting to observe how place-names like this perpetuate the memory of bygone means of travel.

The old ferry at Tal-y-cafn, Dyffryn Conwy

GORSEDD

Gorsedd is the name of a village near Whitford (or Chwitffordd) in Flintshire. It is also a word or element that occurs frequently in the names of fields and farms throughout Wales – *Penrorsedd* being one example.

Question people about the meaning of *gorsedd* and you get two answers. It means either (1) the throne of a king or queen, or (2) with a capital *G*, a society or special institution for poets. But these meanings of the word are comparatively late. It's hard to trace *gorsedd* in the sense of 'throne' further back than the fifteenth century – some 500 years ago. As for *Gorsedd* as an institution for poets, the word in that sense is over 200 years old. It was first used by Iolo Morganwg around 1791 for the meetings of poets he'd begun holding.

The word itself is much older, going back to the beginnings of Welsh proper and further still than that. One of the meanings of the word in its ancient usage was 'court' or 'assembly'. It occurs in the sense 'court of judgment' in the Laws of Hywel Dda. Another of its meanings was 'heap of earth', 'cairn', 'hillock' – frequently a hillock where there was a burial place or *tumulus*. (Witness the Gorsedd Arberth of the *Mabinogi*, a hill with 'sacred' connotations, full of mystery.)

There's a connexion between these different meanings, once we bear in mind that it was customary to hold courts on hillocks in the open air – often on hillocks with 'sacred' associations.

In the Gorsedd near Whitford, the meaning is 'hill';

and an ancient grave or tumulus is also situated there. 'Hill' is the meaning too in the name *Yr Orsedd Goch* near Wrexham – a name that was anglicised to give the present-day *Rossett*.

Narberth castle on its 'gorsedd' in Pembrokeshire

HWLFFORDD
(Haverfordwest)

It is difficult for us today, charging cross-country by car or in the train, to appreciate how important fords used to be for the crossing of rivers.

Place-names remind us of this simple fact. Consider for a moment how many Welsh ones you know of which begin in *Rhyd*, or English ones which end in *ford*.

One of the latter names is *Haverford*(west). *Ford* (Welsh *rhyd*) is the heart of it, preceded by the Old English word *haefer*, 'he-goat', 'buck[deer]'. *Haverford* (= Welsh *Rhyd-y-carw*) was the name the English gave to the place where it was possible to ford the river (Western) Cleddau. As regards meaning, the name is not dissimilar to *Hertford*,

The weir on the Cleddau river near the town centre of Haverfordwest

to the north of London – from *hart*, 'stag', 'horned animal', plus *ford*.

In spoken Welsh *Haverford* became *Hawrffordd*, then *Hawlffordd* and *Hwlffordd*. The *r* in the middle of the name changed to *l* – a change that can occur when two *r*'s come near each other in a word. It was the same sort of change that caused the English words *corner* and *dresser* to become *cornel* and *dresel* in Welsh.

Ford at the end of *Haverford* became *ffordd*: hence *Hwlffordd* in Welsh (compare *Hereford*, Welsh *Henffordd*).In fact our Welsh word *ffordd*, 'road', 'way' is a borrowing from English *ford*, our *rhyd*. It's a very old borrowing, underlining the importance of fords with regard to travelling and roads (*ffyrdd*) in former times.

KENT near CAERNARFON

Seeing Kent as the name of a farm near Pont-rug, just outside Caernarfon, is not a thing you'd expect. It's easy to understand why someone has suggested that a family from Kent in England came there to live at some time or other, but the fact of the matter is that that explanation is completely wrong.

Turn back to the old forms – in the Land Tax registers in the Gwynedd Archives and in the papers of estates such as Y Faenol. There you will find the name has a very different look to it. The old form was *Cefn Tre Saint*, which is easily explained. *Saint* is one form of the name of the river which flows from Llyn Padarn below Pont-rug to its outlet in Caernarfon. In times gone by *tre(f)* meant 'farm'. So *Tre Saint* would be just right as the name of a farm near the river. Later on, *Cefn Tre Saint* would denote the ridge (*cefn*) of land on the edge of that farm.

Cefntresaint is exactly the kind of descriptive combination you very often find as the name of farms and villages in Wales – compare *Cefn*llanfair in the vicinity of Pwllheli, *Cefn*coedycymer near Merthyr, or *Cefn*brynbrain towards Rhydaman.

In speech *cefn* might change to *cen*, with loss of the *f*. That happened in *Cefntresaint*: somewhere around the end of the eighteenth century it became *Centresaint*. Completely losing sight of the meaning of the first element of the name was the next step. The *t* from the original second element was joined to *Cen* to give *Cent*, and the middle of the name became uncertain. The forms

Cent-ar-Saint and *Cent-y-Saint* occur in documents of around 1780. It was a small step, later, to drop the second part of the name *(saint)* in speech, and soon to forget all about it.

By now *Cent* was the spoken form of the name locally. Someone started writing it with an initial *K* – and there we have the form *Kent* that looks so odd in that region today.

River Saint flows from Llyn Padarn under Pont Mwnwgl-y-llyn

LASTRA

Lastra is a farmhouse near Amlwch in Anglesey, which is now also a guesthouse and restaurant.

Mention the name *Lastra* to local people and they're sure to tell you that it's an abbreviation of *galanastra*, a word meaning 'murder', 'massacre', 'destruction'. Immediately afterwards you'll get a big story about a battle that was fought somewhere in the vicinity of Lastra at some time in the past. It's all exciting and very gory – and completely unfounded. But – you may say – how can I brush aside so speedily the story about a battle? What grounds do I have for rejecting the belief that *Lastra* is a version of *galanastra*?

Quite simply, the answer lies in the old versions of the farm's name. To begin with there's the first edition of the OS map in 1838, where the form is *Lastre*, ending in *-e*. The same form, with final *-e*, occurs in documents of 1520 or 1521.

We may accept that *Lastre* is the true name. Now it's a well-known fact that the word *tref* is frequently written and pronounced *tre* – without the *f*: *cartre*, for example, is often found for *cartref*, 'home', and *hendre* for *hendref*, 'winter dwelling'.* Suppose the same thing has happened in the case of *Lastre*. We may now suggest *Lastref* was the *full* form of the name.

What about its first element? It is fairly obvious that there is lenition here – i.e. that *las* represents *glas*, the *g* having been lenited. That re-creates the name as it once was: *Y Lastref*. Formerly *tref* meant 'homestead', 'dwelling', and that is its meaning in *cartref, hendref* and *pentref*. *Tref* also refers to the land around the dwelling – that is, to the whole farm under the old system.

The land of this particular *tref* near Amlwch was *glas*, 'verdant': green and fertile, good for grazing. Thus it was called *Y Las Dref* or *Y Lastref*. In speech the *f* was lost, and in the vernacular of Anglesey the *e* was also changed to *a*, in accordance with a tendency of the dialect. *Y Lastref* became *Y Lastre* and then *Lastra*. It is an accident, and nothing else, that Lastra happened to sound something like the word *galanastra* in the sense of 'battle'. But the story about the battle is a lot more interesting than the explanation I've given. Therefore people prefer to stick to the story, however ill-founded it may be.

* In the sense of 'established habitation', as distinct from *hafod*, 'summer dwelling' – translator's note

LLANDEILO FERWALLT
(Bishopston)

Llandeilo Ferwallt – the English Bishopston – is a village in the Gower Peninsula. Tracing the name of the place tells us quite a lot about the history of the Church in the region.

Llan Merwall or *Llanferwall* was the name of the church here in early times. It was an important religious centre. *Llanferwall* was a combination of *llan* ('church') and *Merwall*, the name of some religious leader with a close connexion to the church – possibly an abbot or senior clergyman. Later on a *t* developed after the *ll* at the end of the name, perhaps owing to the unconscious influence of the word *allt* ('slope', 'hillside'). So Llanferwall became Llanferwallt.

In the course of a heated dispute between Llandaf and Tyddewi (St David's), Llanferwallt was claimed by Llandaf. The patron saint of Llandaf was – and is – Saint Teilo. In order to demonstrate that Llanferwallt belonged to Llandaf, the church was reconsecrated to Teilo and came to be called *Llandeilo Ferwallt*. And that, in Welsh, is always the name for both the parish and the village.

Bishopston, the English name, is a combination of *bishop* and the word *ton* (Old English *tūn*) meaning 'farmstead'. The Bishop of Llandaf owned ecclesiastical land in the parish, so that the 'Bishop's ton' was his farmstead.

LLANRWST

Llanrwst is one of a great many place-names in Wales that begin with *llan*.

The original meaning of the word was 'a piece of land'. It's a very old word, dating back to Brythonic – the ancient tongue from which Welsh sprang – and before that to Celtic, the mother of Brythonic. Ultimately it comes from the same source as the name *Landes* in southern France and the word *land* in English.

Llanrwst bridge, built in 1636

In Welsh, *llan* came to mean a piece of land enclosed for the purpose of keeping something safe. It is present in *perllan*, a piece of land enclosed for cultivating apple-trees, and in *gwinllan*, piece of land for cultivating vines.

Llan also became the Welsh word for a piece of land enclosed and consecrated by one of the early Christian saints for the purpose of building a church, and subsequently it came to signify 'church' on its own. That, for the most part, is its meaning in place-names.

Very often *llan* is followed by the name of an early saint, with the initial consonant of the saint's name being lenited because it is the second element of a compound word – St Teilo in Llandeilo, Tudno in Llandudno and so on. Don't inquire too much about the history of these early saints: we know very little of it as regards most of them.

And *Llanrwst* in Dyffryn Conwy? The old form of the name was *Llanwrwst* – *llan*, 'consecrated land', 'church', plus the saint's name *Gwrwst* – which, in Welsh, corresponds to *Fergus* in Irish. But we know virtually nothing about Gwrwst himself.

MACHYNLLETH

How many of you, I wonder, have noticed the garage in Machynlleth in Montgomeryshire called *Maglona*? If you were to ask people in the town about this name, it's very possible that someone would tell you that it was the old name for Machynlleth used by the Romans.

There is a belief to this effect. It was put forward by the English historian William Camden in the sixteenth century in the great book he wrote concerning Britain, and it has been put forward many times since.

There's no shred of evidence for it. There *was* a Roman town in Britain called *Maglona*, it's true, but that was situated somewhere in the north of England – towards Caerliwelydd (Carlisle) in the opinion of modern scholars.

The *ma* or *mag* at the beginning of the name *Maglona* is identical with the initial *Ma* of *Machynlleth*. It's an old Brythonic word meaning 'plain', 'open land'. On its own like that, *ma* is no longer a word in Welsh, but followed by the ending *-es* it remains in *maes* ('plain', 'field'). It also remains, lenited to *-fa*, in *porfa*, 'pasture for animals to graze', in *morfa*, 'open land near the sea', and so on.

Thus *Machynlleth* was the name for open land on the banks of the river Dyfi. At some period this land was owned by someone named *Cynllaith*, and the site itself came to be called *Machynllaith*.

In the dialect of this part of Wales the *ai* in the last syllable has become *e* – *gobaith* ('hope'), for example, being pronounced *gobeth* – and *Machynllaith* became *Machynlleth*.

Note, too, that the initial *c* of *Cynllaith* is aspirated to *ch*. The same thing occurs in *Mechain* – name of an old *cantref* ('hundred') in Montgomeryshire. That name denotes the plain where the river Cain flows today – *ma-Cain* changing to *Machain* or *Mechain*.

Other place-names in this part of Wales beginning with *ma* are *Mathafarn*, *Mathrafal* and *Mallwyd*. Sir Ifor Williams said that *Mathafarn* referred to the field of some tavern (*tafarn*) or other. This is correct, as long as we remember that *tafarn* signified a place where any sort of commodity was sold – not just food and drink.

Tryfal or *trafal* was the expression for a triangular piece of land at the confluence of two rivers. *Mathrafal* fits the bill exactly – the plain or open land between the rivers Efyrnwy and Banw where the principal court of the kings of Powys was situated. And *Mallwyd*? That could denote a grey-coloured plain, or a plain belonging to some one called Llwyd.

MERTHYR, BASALEG, RADYR

Merthyr, with a small initial *m*, is the Welsh word for a man who suffers death on account of his convictions. More particularly, and in the historical context, *merthyr* – 'martyr' – refers to a person who was put to death for being a Christian. But we need to reflect a little before jumping to the conclusion that *Merthyr* as a place-name – with a capital *M* – refers to a location where someone was martyred.

There used to be another meaning to *merthyr*. As well as denoting a person who died for refusing to renounce Christianity, it was also the word for a building erected in the distant past near the grave of some local Christian leader.

It is this second meaning of *merthyr* which applies to more than one place-name in Wales – to *Merthyr Cynog*, for example, on the fringes of Epynt (the mountain) in Breconshire, and to *Merthyr Mawr* – earlier *Merthyr Myfor* – in the Vale of Glamorgan. In these names *merthyr* refers to some edifice or small church which was erected above the graves of Cynog and Myfor, or else near a graveyard consecrated by their bones. The meaning is the same in *Merthyr Caffo*, an old form of the name *Llangaffo* in Anglesey. And that's the explanation of *Merthyr Tudful*: burial place of a sanctified man or woman named Tudful, or place where his or her bones are believed to be.

The word *merthyr* in this latter sense was borrowed into Welsh from the Latin *martyrium*. It is one of several Latin words borrowed at an early stage for different types of Christian buildings. There's the word *eglwys* ('church') itself, which comes from the Latin *ecclesia*. And then there's the Latin *basilica*: that gave the Welsh word which occurs in the name *Basaleg*, near Newport. Another borrowing from Latin is *oratorium*, which provided the English with the word *oratory* for a small chapel; a Welsh version of that occurs in the name *Radyr*, on the outskirts of Cardiff.

NANT FFRANCON

Nant Ffrancon is the name of the valley in Eryri (Snowdonia) that extends upwards from Bethesda to the pass between Tryfan and Pen yr Ole Wen at the head of Llyn Ogwen. According to Sir Ifor Williams, in his little classic of a book *Enwau Lleoedd* ('Place-names'), what we have here is the old, old word *Ffranc* meaning 'hired soldier' – that is, a mercenary.

A *Ffranc*, of course (English *Frank*) was a member of the Germanic people who conquered Gaul around 500 AD and who gave their name to *France* ('Frankland') and to *Frenchmen* ('Frankishmen').

Some of these Germanic Franks, said Sir Ifor, used to come over to fight for pay in Wales during the centuries, more than a thousand years ago, before the Normans. *Ffranc* was the term for one of these foreign soldiers, *Ffrancon* denoting more than one of them – the plural termination – *on* being the same as in *Saeson* ('Englishmen'), *lladron* ('robbers') etc. Then Sir Ifor conjectured that a band of these mercenaries – a band of Franks – were rewarded by some chieftain in Gwynedd who settled them in *Nant Ffrancon*.

It's an agreeable and plausible explanation. But subsequently, in the periodical *Notes and Queries*, a scholar named Andrew Breeze from the University of Navarre in Spain offered an alternative one. There was a word *ffranca* in Old English meaning 'spear', and according to Andrew Breeze this word was borrowed into Welsh with the same meaning – just as *tarian*, 'shield' was borrowed from the same source. According to this explanation, the meaning of *Nant Ffrancon* is 'valley of the spears', and not 'valley where Frankish soldiers were settled'.

In support of this explanation Breeze cites a line from an old Welsh poem of around the year 900. In it, a Welsh lord is sitting before a cauldron or crock pouring out his sorrows. He has lost his army, and sits there alone and disheartened. 'I and my *ffranc* around our cauldron,' says the poem. For Sir Ifor, the poem pictures the Welsh lord with no one for company but a Frankish soldier. No, says Breeze. The lord is here with no one at all, only his spear – his *ffranc* – for company. It is a sad picture, like that of Llywarch Hen – an old man low in spirit and leaning on his staff or 'wooden crook' – in another early Welsh poem.

The 'U' shaped valley of Nant Ffrancon

NANTLLE

Nantlle, in Gwynedd, in that form, is the name seen on signposts, and the spoken form is *Nantlle* or *Nanlle*. But its full form is *Nant Lleu*: that is, 'Lleu's Valley', which immediately suggests all sorts of connexions.

Lleu is the name of the central character in the Fourth Branch of the *Mabinogi*. In this old tale it is related of him that, after being betrayed by his wife Blodeuwedd, he turns into an eagle and flies away. The magician Gwydion finds him in the oak wood of Dyffryn Nantlle and turns him back into a man.

The name *Lleu* is interesting. At root it's identical with the *lleu* which is the first part of *lleuad* ('moon') and the second part of *golau*, 'light'. Trace the word behind it to Brythonic – the Celtic language from which Welsh sprang – and still further to the Celtic dialects which were spoken across extensive parts of Europe before the Romans, and you come to the form *lug* – a word cognate with *lux*, which means 'light' in Latin.

Lugus, god of light, was one of the leading divinities of the ancient Celts. When they named a fort or important town, they often did so in his honour, calling it 'dinas Lleu' – or rather, according to the usage of their language at the time, *Lugudunum*. There was more than one town of this name on the Continent, and as the language of each area changed in the course of hundreds and hundreds of years so the name changed also. In the south of France it became *Lyon*, in northern France *Laon*, and in Holland *Leyden*. Every one of these towns was originally a stronghold dedicated to the Celtic god *Lugus*, or *Lleu*.

Returning to *Lugudunum* for a moment, I said that *lug* has become *lleu* in Welsh and that *dun* has become *din*, as in *dinas* ('city'). Given the existence of a *Lugudunum* in Wales, you would expect it to have developed into *Lleudin*. Take this name and reverse the order of its elements and there you have *Dinlleu*. It is the ancient fort Dinas Dinlle in the vicinity of Caernarfon, not far from Nantlle.

Place-names often speak volumes, and names like *Nantlle* and *Dinas Dinlle* certainly do that. They whisper to us of the ancient Celtic god *Lleu*, whose powers were venerated by our ancestors 2,500 years ago.

Looking eastwards along Nantlle valley towards Snowdon summit

PENCHWINTAN

Penchwintan is the name of a part of Bangor – the part where you go up the hill towards Penrhosgarnedd and Ysbyty Gwynedd. Near Abergeirw in Meirionnydd, between Llanfachreth and Trawsfynydd, you find *Adwychwintan* and *Brynchwintan*, while in Llandecwyn in Ardudwy there's a hill called *Talarchwintan*.

The word *chwintan* is an interesting one. Ultimately it's a borrowing of the French *quintaine*, which gave *quintain* in English and which denoted a pole stuck upright into the ground. In olden times it was the custom among mounted knights and foot soldiers to charge towards the pole and attack it with lances or staves. Sometimes a sack filled with sand was suspended on an arm of the quintain or pole, and the trick then was to attack the sack with the same weapons. It was all a kind of military training.

Long after the days of armed knights, attacking the quintain continued as a popular sport among country folk – especially as part of the jollity in celebration of a wedding. The custom was for the bridegroom and his friends to attack the quintain with staves. The one who broke most staves on the quintain was champion of the games. This kind of sport was still going strong in Shrewsbury in the eighteenth century: William Owen Pughe, in his dictionary of 1793, describes the custom himself. It is the memory of some old country sport like this that is preserved in the names Penchwintan, Brynchwintan and Talarchwintan.

In south-western Wales, *cwinten* is the form of the word *chwintan*. There, it lives on to denote the custom of placing a rope across the road to stop the car of a newly-married couple while demanding a 'toll' – *ffwtin* in Welsh – to let them pass.

PENTYRCH

There is more than one *Pentyrch*. There's a *Pen-tyrch* village (pronounced as spelt) in the outskirts of Cardiff; *Bentyrch* in the region of Llanfair Caereinion in Montgomeryshire, also *Bentyrch* and a mountain, *Garn Bentyrch*, in Eifionydd. And in Monmouthshire, in the vicinity of Tyndyrn (Tintern), there's a farm called *Penteri* today, its old form being *Pen-tyrch*. All these are very old names, going far back to the Middle Ages; they are referred to in documents of 1300-1350.

Each consists of *pen* ('head') plus a form of the word *twrch* ('wild pig'). But why the form *tyrch*? Dealing earlier with the name *Caerdydd* (Cardiff) I said that originally the second element was *Tyf*, a genitival form of *Taf* – i.e. the original meaning of Caerdydd was 'the fort of the Taf'.

The form *Pentyrch* is similar, *tyrch* being an old genitival form of *twrch*. So in the beginning the meaning of *Pentyrch* was *'pen y twrch* – 'boar's head'.

It's possible to accept that names like *Pentyrch* describe some geographical feature – that there is a hillock or rock whose shape resembles the head of a pig or boar wherever you have the name. And it's possible to explain *Pen-houch* (Pen-hwch) in Brittany and *Swineshead* in England in the same way. But recent scholars incline towards another – and different – explanation.

Many centuries ago people in a cantref (hundred) or district would assemble at special meeting places in the open air. In these places it was customary to fix the head of an animal on a pole – like a totem pole. It's very likely that there was once a boar's head on a pole marking an early meeting place in each one of the four *Pentyrch* or *Bentyrch* in Wales.

Y BONT-FAEN; PEN-Y-BONT
(Cowbridge; Bridgend)

Bridges have had an enormous effect on the settlements, economy, politics – and place-names – of Wales. In saying this I'm not referring to large, impressive structures such as the one over the Severn, or the Menai Bridge; I'm thinking rather of the hundreds of much smaller and older bridges that made it possible for our long-gone ancestors to travel across the country to the market and the fair.*

One useful aid in seeking to frame a map of these old bridges is place-names containing the word *pont* – for example names like the *Pen-y-bont ar Ogwr* ('end of the bridge on the river Ogwr') and *Y Bont-faen* ('the bridge of stone') of the title.

There was a bridge in the locality of Y Bont-faen well over 700 years ago, somewhere near the place where the old Roman road from Cardiff to Neath crossed the river Ddawan (Thaw). In documents of 1262-1263 there was a reference to the place under the name Covbruge/Coubrigge, the Old English forms of Cowbridge, or bridge for cows.

What sort of bridge was it, I wonder, and why was it called Cowbridge? I don't know the answer. But around it, in the fourteenth century, grew up one of the largest towns in Wales. Later on, another bridge was built – a stone one; and this gave us the Welsh name, Y Bont-faen ('the bridge of stone'), which occurs around 1500.

Pen-y-bont ar Ogwr is considerably 'younger' as a

place than Y Bont-faen. In the Middle Ages there is no mention of it. There were two settlements or villages – Newcastle towards the west and Nolton or Oldcastle towards the east, with the river Ogwr in between them.

Somewhere around 1435 or a little afterwards a four-arched bridge was constructed. Soon a few houses went up at its eastern end, and these came to be called *Bridgend* – or (in Welsh) *Pen-y-bont*. It was a very small place until the post-1820 industrialisation. After that Pen-y-bont grew swiftly, swallowing up Newcastle and Nolton.

* An excellent guide to these is Gwyndaf Breese's *The Bridges of Wales* (Gwasg Carreg Gwalch, 2001) – translator's note

PONT-IETS
(Pont Yates)

Pont-iets is a village to the north of Llanelli. On looking at the name, written like that, it would be easy to start thinking of the word *iet* which is heard in parts of western Wales for *giât* ('gate'). But it would be a mistake to follow that trail.

You often see *Pont-Yates* on maps, and that form is a little nearer the mark as regards explaining the name. *Pont* ('bridge') and the English surname *Yates* is what we have here. The name *Pont Yates* occurs in Emanuel Bowen's 1760 map of southern Wales – the earliest reference to it as far as I know. But earlier than that, in 1739, there is a reference to a house called *Tŷ iets* in the area. Mr Dilwyn Roberts of Pont-iets mentioned this to me; he had spotted a reference to it in an old document. Mr Roberts also observed that a man called Walter Yates was living in the parish of Llangyndeyrn in the period 1642-66. All this is an excellent example of the value of precise knowledge of local history in explaining place-names.

Thanks to Mr Roberts's researches it's now possible to trace the name *Pont-iets* with a fair degree of certainty. 350 years ago a certain man called Yates came to live in the area. The house (*tŷ*) specially associated with him or with his family was called *Tŷ Yates* – or Tŷ-iets in the vernacular. A bridge was built nearby. This was called *Pont Tŷ iets*, and that was simplified to *Pont-iets*.

By the way, the joining of a personal name or surname with the word *pont* is a common enough custom. There are *Pontantawn* (from *pont* and the Welsh version of *Antony*); *Pont-henri* and *Pontabram* in the same area (Llangyndeyrn); *Pont-siân* near Llandysul; *Pontrobert* in Ann Griffiths* country in Montgomeryshire; and several others.

* Welsh poet and hymn-writer, 1776-1805; author of the words 'Wele'n sefyll rhwng y myrtwydd' (English version: 'Bread of Heaven') which are sung on the tune *Cwm Rhondda*

                                                     – translator's note

PONT-Y-PŴL (Pontypool), PONTYPRIDD

Superficially these two names appear to be of the same type – a combination of *pont* + the particle *y* + another monosyllable. But in fact the resemblance is deceptive.

I know there are some who suggest that Pontypŵl is a corrupt form of *Pont ap Hywel*, but there is not a shred of evidence to support this. *Pont-y-pŵl* is a simple combination of *pont*, 'bridge' and the English word 'pool'. The meaning is 'bridge where there was a pool' – the pool probably referring to a pool in the river Llwyd.

What about *Pontypridd*? The first thing to note that this is not *pont* + *y* + *pridd* ('earth'). *Pont-y-tŷ-pridd* was the old form of the name – in documents of around 1700, for example. A house with earthen walls formerly stood at

The old stone-arched bridge at Pontypridd

one end of the bridge, and it was that house which gave its name to the old bridge itself.

Try pronouncing *Pont-y-tŷ-pridd* fairly quickly. Inevitably you will contract the middle part and say *Pontypridd*.

Between 1746 and 1755 the Independent minister William Edwards built a new bridge here – the striking and well-known one with a single arch. Naturally, there were some who called this new structure *New Bridge*, which could easily have become the name of the town which grew up here. But this didn't happen, probably because there was another Newbridge – and the name *Pontypridd* survived.

PORTHAETHWY
(Menai Bridge)

The name *Pont y Borth* comes naturally to me when speaking of Thomas Telford's famous structure over the Menai Strait. It was 'Pont y Borth' that I heard as a child, and that's the term used by the people of Anglesey ever since the building of the bridge was completed in 1826.

Y Borth is the colloquial name among Anglesey folk for the town of *Porthaethwy*. It was the English who christened Telford's structure *Menai Bridge*, and who subsequently – by way of extension – used that as a new name for Porthaethwy. Thus Menai Bridge is a late name – a century and a half old at most. Porthaethwy is older by some 1500 years.

At first glance it's a combination of *porth* ('port', 'ferry-point') and a second element *Aethwy*. Or so some believed in the nineteenth century. As a result, when Anglesey was divided into local government districts in 1894, one of the districts was called *Aethwy*. But in point of fact, the name was completely spurious.

The old name for this part of Anglesey in the Middle Ages was *Dindaethwy* – a combination of *din*, 'fort' – as we see in Dinbych (Denbigh) – and the element *Daethwy*. And the latter? That's one of the names in Early Welsh ending in *-wy* used to denote a tribe of people, or the piece of land belonging to that particular tribe. Another example was *Deganwy*, i.e. land of the people called *Decanae* by the Romans.

Daethwy was the name of a British tribe living on the

108

banks of the Menai Strait. The fort which served as their centre was *Dindaethwy* – probably the fort now called *Dinas*, near Plas Cadnant.

Among the possessions of this tribe was the site used for crossing from Anglesey to the mainland in Arfon. That site came to be called *Porthddaethwy* ('Ferry-point of the Daethwy'). In speech the *dd* was absorbed by the *th* preceding it. *Porthddaethwy* naturally became *Porthaethwy*, later shortened colloquially to *Borth*. After all, this was *the* most important ferry-point (*porth*) for crossing the Menai Strait.

Pont y Borth, connecting Anglesey and the mainland

PORTH-CAWL

Who would imagine that the *cawl* in the name *Porth-cawl* in Glamorgan is the same as the *cawl* ('cabbage') that we eat for dinner? Yet that's the fact of the matter. The word *cawl* was borrowed into Welsh from the Latin *caulis*, a word for a cabbage stalk. It was ultimately the same Latin word that gave the English the *cauli* in 'cauliflower', the *cole* in 'cole-slaw', and also the word 'kale'.

In Welsh, *cawl* can mean 'cabbage' (*bresych, cabaetsen*). It also occurs in a word for a kind of broth containing this plant.

There is another plant which the English call 'sea-kale' and which grows near seashores. In his *Welsh Botanology* of 1813, Hugh Davies says that it is to be found on the shore in Penmon and Llanddona (Anglesey), but adds that it's a fairly rare plant.

There must be a lot of 'sea kale' growing on the shore in Drenewydd yn Notais (Newton Nottage), Glamorgan. *Cawl* or *cawl môr* used to be the name for it. The harbour or seashore where this was plentiful came to be called *Porth-cawl* – exactly as the shore at Llanfwrog in Anglesey came to be called *Porthdelysg* – because a kind of edible seaweed, *delysg*, was to be found there. Incidentally, it's thought that the stalk of sea-kale is tasty to eat.

PRESTATYN

Prestatyn in Flintshire stands on the threshold of the Vale of Clwyd (Dyffryn Clwyd), a good twenty-five miles from Chester and the boundary between Wales and England. You would scarcely expect to find a 1000-year-old English name in such a locality, but that's the case here. Prestatyn is an English name – or rather the Welsh form of its original in the Old English tongue.

It goes back to the Old English *Prēosta-tūn* – *prēosta* being a plural meaning '(of the) priests' and *tūn* meaning 'estate' or 'farm'. *Tūn*, incidentally, is one of the elements that occur most frequently in English place-names – in Bol*ton*, Brigh*ton*, Lu*ton*, Wal*ton*, and so on.

During the seventh and eighth centuries Englishmen from Mercia pushed into north-east Wales – into the vicinity of Wrexham and up the river Alun towards Yr Wyddgrug (Mold), and along the coast from Chester towards Penarlâg (Hawarden) and Prestatyn. Old English names like Wrexham, Mold, Northop and Hawarden are relics of that early incursion. And there is also Prestatyn. Land in this place was given over to priests, or to support priests, and was called *Prēosta-tūn*, 'Priests' Farm'.

Something similar occurred in Lancashire on the estuary of the Ribble. There too a farm or estate for priests was established; but that *Prēosta-tūn* developed naturally into Preston, in accordance with the essential characteristics of change of the English language. It didn't happen like this in Flintshire: there the name was *Prēosta-tūn* in the beginning, with the accent on the last syllable, *tūn*. But the place was a tiny island of English in the middle of fluent Welsh-speakers, and because of this its name acquired a Welsh pronunciation.

This meant placing the accent on the penultimate syllable, rather than on the ultimate – which meant pronouncing *Prēosta-tūn* as *Prestátyn*, with the accent on the *a*. That is why the *a* that was lost in *Preston* came to be retained. And that is why I said that *Prestatyn* is the Welsh form of an old English name.

Prestatyn beach

Rhuddlan castle

RHUDDLAN and RHUTHUN (Ruthin)

In one of the earliest chronicles dealing with the history of Wales that has been preserved for us, there is a mention of the *bellum Rudglann*, 'battle of Rhuddlan'. Around this battle grew up the later story of the Massacre of the Rhuddlan Marsh, and the apocryphal tale which claims that the sad folk-song 'Morfa Rhuddlan' ('marsh of Rhuddlan') was composed in the wake of a Welsh defeat by the English at the time in question.

Rudglann, let it be noted, is the form of the name in the old chronicle. This early way of spelling it clearly shows that it's a combination of the adjective *rhudd*, 'red' and the noun *glan*, 'bank or edge of a river'; and the soil in the

Vale of Clwyd is of a reddish colour.

The same *rhudd*, 'red' is the first element of the name *Rhuthun* higher up the valley (*dyffryn*). But what about its second element? It is often said that this is the word *din*, 'fort' – the same *din* as that at the end of *Caerfyrddin*. That's the opinion of Sir J. E. Lloyd in his two great volumes on the history of Wales. He frequently mentions 'the red fort occupying a ridge of red sandstone' – that is, Rhuthun is seen as a later form of an old *Rhudd-ddin*.

But there is a problem connected with this explanation. *Rhudd* ends with the 'soft' consonant *dd*, and the same soft consonant, *dd*, would be at the beginning of

Ruthin town square

114

ddin in the second element. Now you would not expect two *dd* sounds like these to combine as *th*, any more than two *dd*'s would correspond to *th* in a line conforming to the *cynghanedd*.*

There is another possibility, as Sir Ifor Williams has suggested. Soft *dd* could be followed by *h*, to give the sound *th* quite naturally. You will guess, therefore, that *rhudd + hin* was the original form here. This gave Rhuthin to begin with, and then – through the colouring of the *i* at the end by the *u* in the first part – Rhuthun.

A word *hin* existed in the early period of Welsh that meant 'side', 'edge', 'boundary'. It is still seen in *(r)hiniog*, an extant expression for the piece of wood on the ground across the threshold of a door. In reality *rhiniog* is *yr hiniog* – 'edge', 'boundary'. And 'side' is its meaning in the names *Rhinog Fawr* and *Rhinog Fach*, denoting the two mountains that stand like doorposts on either side of the Drws Ardudwy pass in Meirionnydd. Their mountain range is named after those two peaks – the *Rhinogydd*.

The meaning of *Ruthun*, from *Rhudd + hin*, may be 'reddish edge', a reference to the face of the sandstone rock or else to the bank of the river (Clwyd). Assuming this, we see that the meanings of *Rhuthun* (Denbighshire) and *Rhuddlan* (Flintshire) are very similar.

* The rules of metrical consonance in Welsh verse – translator's note

Y RHYL
(Rhyl)

Y Rhyl is one of the most popular coastal towns in northern Wales. The name is an old one, at all events going back 700 years. There is a reference in 1301 to *Ryhull*, to *del Hull* in 1302, *Hullhouse* in 1351, *Yrhill* in 1578, *Tre-yr-hyll* in 1612 and *Rhyll* in 1660.

What we have here in all probability is the English word *hill* (also meaning hillock) in its Old English form *hyll* or else in one if its Middle English forms. We can compare it with the *hull* of *Solihull* in Birmingham – *hull* here being a form for *hill*.

But wait a moment, some of you may say. The *hull* in Solihull refers to quite a sizeable 'hillock' – i.e. the hill to the south of the church – whereas the *Rhyl* in northern Wales is situated in a flat plain, without a hillock near it. True, in the strict geographical sense. But before rejecting the above ('hill', 'hillock') explanation, consider this – that *hyll* or *hull* in English could mean a quite small rise of land in the middle of a plain.

It's possible that that was the original meaning of the *Rhyl* in Flintshire. The early English referred to the rise of land towards the mouth of the river Clwyd as a *hull*, and before long *Hull* became the name of the spot. This name was adopted by the Welsh inhabitants of the area, and the Welsh definite article *yr* was added in front of it. *Hull* became *Yr hull* or *Yr hill* and then *Rhyl* – that is, a half-'cymricised' English name.

Rhyl

There are other examples of *(y)r*, the definite article, joined to the beginning of place-names – *Rachub*, the name of a village near Bethesda, being one. The word *achub*, in the sense 'landholding', is the source of *Rachub*. The piece of land in question was called *Yr Achub*, which was contracted in the spoken tongue to *Rachub*.

TREBANWS
(Trebanos)

Trebanws is a village in the Tawe valley, Glamorgan.

The earlier name was *Trebanos*. That's what you see in a document of 1590 in which the Earl of Worcester complains that certain of his tenants have appropriated lands belonging to him, including 30 acres 'from a place called Tree Bannos'. (The document was printed in the 1968 number of the *Bulletin of the Board of Celtic Studies*, and is sprinkled with names from the Swansea – Abertawe – area.)

The first element of Trebanws is *tre* or *tref* in its old sense of farmstead, or dwelling-place of the head of a family and his sons. It's the same *tref* as in *cartref* ('home') and *hendref* ('established habitation'), and is a very common element in Welsh place-names. But what about the *banos* which is used descriptively of *tre*(f) here?

The first thing to remember is that more often than not there is soft mutation (lenition) in the first element that follows *tre* – for example in *Tredegar* ('home of Tegyr') and *Tregaron* ('farmstead on the river Caron'). The task, then, is to seek a word 'panos' in order to explain the name *Trebanos*.

There is a plural termination *os* which frequently occurs with the names of plants in Welsh place-names. There's *grugos*, for a place abounding with heather. Add *y* in front of it and you have *Y Rugos* – i.e. *Y Rhigos* in Glamorgan.

Another example is *bedwos*, a word for a copse of

Tregaron

young birch trees, which occurs in *Bedwas* near Caerphilly. Add to these two *Y Wernos*, the name of a coal mine near Rhydaman where there were a lot of young alders (*gwern*), and Lygos – from Helygos,* the name of a farm above the Clydach.

There's a word *pân* signifying 'cotton grass'. From *pân* you get the form *panos* that occurs in *Trebanos*. That farm was once on meadowland where the cotton grass was thick in season.

* From *helyg*, 'willows' – translator's note

TREFYCLO and LLANANDRAS
(Knighton and Presteigne)

Trefyclo and Llandandras – Knighton and Presteigne in English – are border towns in Radnorshire. The name *Trefyclo* states that clearly enough: the old form was *Trefyclawdd* – i.e. the town that was on Offa's Dyke (*Clawdd*).

It seems that the name was originally *Tref-y-Clawdd*, in three parts, but in the course of time it came to be pronounced as a single word with the accent on the *y*, in accordance with the Welsh language custom of accenting the penultimate syllable. The next natural step was the dropping of the final soft *dd* and the sounding of the *aw* as *o*. *Trefyclawdd* became *Trefýclo*, just as *Abermawdd* became *Abérmo* or *Bermo*.

Its English name *Knighton* is very old, going back a thousand years. It is a combination of two Old English words – *cniht*, meaning 'servant' or 'soldier', and *tūn*, 'farm' etc., which gave *ton* at the end of so many English place-names.

'Town of the soldiers' was the original meaning of Knighton. Incidentally, the same English word *cniht* – the old form of 'knight' – gave the *Cnicht* mountain in Meirionnydd its name: the shape of it resembles a knight's helmet.

And Presteigne? In 1278 that was recorded in the form *Presthemede* – with *m*, that is, and not *n*, in its final part. *Prēost*, the Old English for 'priest', is the first element while *hemede* in the second represents *haemed*, an Old

English variant of the word *hām*, later 'home', with the termination *-ed*. Thus the name meant 'home or household of the priest', which is very similar to the meaning of *Prestatyn* and *Preston*. With the passage of time *Presthemede* changed to *Presteigne* in spoken English.

In Welsh the place is called *Llanandras* – *llan*, 'church', and *Andras* or *Andreas*, the name of the brother of Simon Peter who was the first of the disciples, according to the Gospels. *Andreas* was a very popular saint in the Middle Ages, and he was the Andrew who became the patron saint of Scotland. In England, more than 600 churches have been dedicated to him, while in Wales he is to be found in the parish of *St Andrews* (or *Sant Andras*) in the hundred of Dinas Powys, as well as in the Radnorshire *Llanandras*.

Llannau place-names which include the names of Biblical saints are usually much later than those dedicated to Welsh saints such as Dewi, Teilo, Tudno, Elli, etc.

Knighton

TREGANNA
(Canton)

In 1901 there were 12,395 Welsh-speakers in Cardiff. By the time of the 1981 census the figure was 14,245. In 1981 the percentage of Welsh-speakers in Cardiff was higher than at any time since the First World War. And one of the districts where there was an increase was *Canton* or *Treganna*.

To you and me today, *tref* or *tre* is the Welsh word corresponding to 'town' in English. But the old meaning of *tref* was 'homestead' or 'farmstead' – the house in which the family lived plus the surrounding land.

That is the meaning of *tref* in the second part of *cartref* – homestead of the *câr* or family. That is also its meaning in *hendref* and in *pentref*. (Originally, *pentref* was the end – *pen* – of the farmstead or estate where dwelt the men bound to the land and to their lord.)

In the region of Bodorgan in Anglesey there is a mansion called *Trefeilyr*. This was probably the homestead or farmstead gifted by one of the Welsh princes to the court poet Meilyr. Not far from Trefeilyr was *Trewalchmai*, the homestead gifted to the poet Gwalchmai. Trewalchmai, lacking the initial *tre*, still survives in the name of the village, *Gwalchmai* – the only village I know of to be named after the poet, though there is nothing there today to remind us of him except the sign above the inn.

In *Trefeilyr* and *Trewalchmai* a personal name follows *tre*. That pattern – *tre(f)* + personal name – is a common one in place-names. And that is what we have in *Treganna*. At the outset *Treganna* was the *tre* – farmstead or estate – of someone named *Canna*.

And *Canton*? That begins with the same personal name *Canna* or *Cann*. The second part is *ton* or *tūn*, an English word very similar to *tref* as regards meaning, and one of the most common elements in English place-names.

Which one came first, the English *Canton* or *Treganna*? There's no way of answering for sure. A record exists of the English form *Canetune* from the year 1230, much earlier than the recording of the Welsh form. It's very likely that *Canton* is the earlier form and that it was 'cymricised' to *Treganna*. Today, certainly, *Treganna* is regaining its place once more.

Trefeilyr, Anglesey

TRELAWNYD
(Newmarket)

What do you make of *Trelawnyd*, the name of a village near Prestatyn in Flintshire? Not much, I suspect, on the basis of the name as it exists today.

Trelawnyd is one of those names that have changed greatly over the centuries. It is mentioned in Domesday Book, that great land survey carried out at the request of the English king.

There you see *Rivelenoit* – the attempt of the clerk who framed the entry to record *Rhiwlyfnwyd*. That was the old name: *rhiw*, signifying 'hillside' – *allt* in northern Wales – followed perhaps by a personal name *Llyfnwyd*.

At some time or other *Rhiwlyfnwyd* became *Trelyfnwyd* – which later, in speech, became something like *Trelynwyd* (with loss of the *f*) and later still *Trelawnyd*. At least, that's one way of attempting to make sense of the strange forms that exist for the name.

Around the year 1700 support began for a new market there that gave rise to the name *Newmarket* – the English name for Trelawnyd.

WRECSAM
(Wrexham)

Wrecsam is the largest town in northern Wales. And it is one in which I have a personal interest, for it was in Wrecsam that I was born.

Here am I having already written the name twice as though it were Welsh, putting *cs* in the middle of it instead of the English *xh*. But I have every right to do that. The Welsh form *Gwregsam* occurs as early as 1291 – more than seven centuries ago!

But the name has an English origin. The English came to this area early on: Wansdyke and Offa's Dyke were built to the west of Wrexham in the eighth century to mark the boundary of the Mercian English kings, and it is reasonable to infer that the name Wrexham itself goes back to that remote period, a thousand years ago and more, when the English were settling in the region.

What about the source of the name? It's possible that the last part consists of the Old English word *hamm** as in Evesham and West Ham. That was the opinion of Professor Melville Richards, for example. But it is also possible that the Old English *hām* meaning 'settlement', 'village' – as at the end of Birmingham – features here.

And the first element? Although the earliest written forms of the name – *Wristlesham*, for example, in 1161 – vary somewhat, there is a general consensus that what is here is the Old English personal name *Wryhtel*. Basically, then, *Wrexham* represents the Old English for a meadow or good grazing land belonging to someone called

Wryhtel, or else the name of some kind of early English village connected with him. But although the English had possession of the region and left their mark on place-names there, the Welsh did not entirely lose their grip on the place. And Wrexham was 'cymricised' to *Gwrecsam*.

The two forms of the name – Wrexham and Wrecsam – preserve the memory of much of the past history of this border region.

* *Hamm*, 'meadow' – translator's note

Wrexham

Index

Further Reading

Charles, B. G. (1938)
Non-Celtic Place-Names in Wales
(University College London)

Davies, Elwyn (1957, 1967)
Rhestr o Enwau Lleoedd/A Gazetteer of Welsh Place-Names
(University of Wales Press, Cardiff)

John, D. (1998)
Cynon Valley Place-Names
(Gwasg Carreg Gwalch, Llanrwst)

John, D. (1999)
Notes on some Placenames in and around the Bont
(Deric John, Aberdare)

Jones, B. L. and Roberts, T. (1979)
'Coastal toponyms of Anglesey' in *Journal of the English Place-Name Society 11*

Jones, B. L. (1991)
'Place-names: Signposts to the past in Anglesey' in *Transactions of the Anglesey Antiquarian Society and Field Club* 23-37

Jones, G. T. and Roberts, T. (1996)
Enwau Lleoedd Môn/The Place-Names of Anglesey
(Isle of Anglesey County Council, Research Centre Wales, Bangor University)

Leaver, T. (1998)
Pronouncing Welsh Place Names
(Gwasg Carreg Gwalch, Llanrwst)

Lias, A. (1994)
A Guide to Welsh Place-Names
(Gwasg Carreg Gwalch, Llanrwst)

Lewis, D. G. (2007)
Y Llyfr Enwau: Enwau'r Wlad. A Check-list of Welsh Place-Names (Gomer, Llandysul)

Morgan, R. with Evans, G. G. (1993)
Enwau Lleoedd Buallt a Maesyfed
(Gwasg Carreg Gwalch, Llanrwst)

Morgan, R. (1998)
A Study of Radnorshire Place-Names
(Gwasg Carreg Gwalch, Llanrwst)

Morgan, R. and Powell, R. F. P. (1999)
A Study of Breconshire Place-Names
(Gwasg Carreg Gwalch, Llanrwst)

Morgan, R. (2001)
A Study of Montgomeryshire Place-Names
(Gwasg Carreg Gwalch, Llanrwst)

Morgan, R. (2005)
Place-names of Gwent (Gwasg Carreg Gwalch, Llanrwst)

Ordnance Survey (2004)
A Glossary of the most common Welsh elements used on maps of Wales (Southampton)

Osborne, G. and Hobbs, G. (1998)
The Place-Names of Eastern Gwent
(Old Bakehouse, Abertillery)

Osborne, G. and Hobbs, G. (2002)
The Place-Names of Western Gwent
(Old Bakehouse, Abertillery)

Owen, H. W. (1987)
'English place-names and Welsh stress-patterns' in
Nomina XI, 99-114 ed. C. Clark, O. J. Padel, A. Rumble, V.
Smart (Society for Name Studies in Britain and Ireland)

Owen, H. W. (1998)
The Place-Names of Wales (University of Wales Press, The
Western Mail, Cardiff)

Owen, H. W. and Morgan, R. (2007)
Dictionary of the Place-names of Wales
(Gwasg Gomer, Ceredigion)

Oxenham, W. (2005)
Welsh Origins of Scottish Place-names
(Gwasg Carreg Gwalch, Llanrwst)

Pierce, G. O. (2002)
Place-Names in Glamorgan (Merton Priory Press, Cardiff)

Pierce, G. O., Roberts, T. and Owen, H.W. (1997)
Ar Draws Gwlad (Gwasg Carreg Gwalch, Llanrwst)

Pierce, G. O. and Roberts, T. (1999)
Ar Draws Gwlad 2 (Gwasg Carreg Gwalch, Llanrwst)

Richards, M. (1998)
Enwau Tir a Gwlad ed. B.L. Jones (Gwasg Gwynedd,
Caernarfon)